iLit

Strength an[d ...]

Perspectives from First Nations, Inuit, and Métis Peoples in Canada

Education Advisors

Rachel A. Mishenene
Anishinaabe
Curriculum Developer
Matawa First Nations Education Department
Thunder Bay, ON

Dr. Pamela Rose Toulouse
Sagamok First Nation
Associate Professor
School of Education, Laurentian University
Sudbury, ON

Reviewers

Denise Augustine
Chemainus First Nation
Curriculum Coordinator
Cowichan Valley School District 79, BC

Nichola Batzel
Inuit
Aboriginal Support Teacher
Winnipeg School Division, MB

Jason EagleSpeaker
Blackfoot-Duwamish
Marketing, Communications & Family Engagement
Aboriginal Education Team
Calgary Board of Education, AB

Starleigh Grass
Tsilhqot'in Nation
Teacher, Lillooet Secondary School
Gold Trail School District 74, BC

Deanna McCallum
Ojibway
Student, Children of the Earth High School
Winnipeg School Division, MB

Chris McLeod
Métis Nation of Ontario
Education Analyst/Officer
Métis Nation of Ontario, ON

Taren Orchard
Ojibway
Student, Children of the Earth High School
Winnipeg School Division, MB

Dr. Angelina Weenie
Plains Cree
Acting Department Head of Professional Programs
First Nations University of Canada, SK

McGraw-Hill Ryerson

Toronto Montréal Boston Burr Ridge, IL Dubuque, IA
Madison, WI New York San Francisco St. Louis Bangkok
Bogotá Caracas Kuala Lumpur Lisbon London Madrid
Mexico City Milan New Delhi Santiago Seoul
Singapore Sydney Taipei

The McGraw-Hill Companies

COPIES OF THIS BOOK MAY BE OBTAINED BY CONTACTING:

McGraw-Hill Ryerson Ltd.

WEB SITE:
http://www.mcgrawhill.ca

E-MAIL:
orders@mcgrawhill.ca

TOLL-FREE FAX:
1-800-463-5885

TOLL-FREE CALL:
1-800-565-5758

OR BY MAILING YOUR ORDER TO:
McGraw-Hill Ryerson
Order Department
300 Water Street
Whitby, ON L1N 9B6

Please quote the ISBN and title when placing your order.

McGraw-Hill Ryerson
Strength and Struggle: Perspectives from First Nations, Inuit, and Métis Peoples in Canada

ISBN 13: 978-0-07-106703-4
ISBN 10: 0-07-106703-5

http://www.mcgrawhill.ca

1 2 3 4 5 6 7 8 9 TCP 1 9 8 7 6 5 4 3 2 1

Printed and bound in Canada

Publisher: Sandra McTavish
Senior Content Manager: Rivka Cranley
Developmental Editor: Megan Robinson
Acquisitions Editor: Jody Porter
Manager, Editorial Services: Crystal Shortt
Supervising Editor: Jeanette McCurdy
Copy Editor: Karen Rolfe
Review Coordinator: Jennifer Keay
Editorial Assistant: Erin Hartley
Manager, Production Services: Yolanda Pigden
Production Coordinator: Tammy Mavroudi
Art Direction: Jodie Bernard, Laserwords Private Ltd.
Electronic Page Make-up: Laserwords Private Ltd.
Photo Research And Permissions: Cynthia Howard
Cover Design: Jodie Bernard, Laserwords Private Ltd.
Cover Image: Moses (Amik) Beaver

About the Education Advisors

Rachel A. Mishenene

Rachel Mishenene is a curriculum developer with Matawa First Nations Education Department in Thunder Bay, Ontario. She has developed Aboriginal education curriculum with the Elementary Teachers' Federation of Ontario, Lakehead University, and Ningwakwe Learning Press.

She is an experienced elementary and secondary teacher and also has extensive teaching practicum within Aboriginal Education at the postsecondary level for pre-service and qualified teachers in Aboriginal education in Ontario.

Rachel is the chair of the Elementary Teachers' Federation of Ontario's Aboriginal Education Committee, as well as the Social Justice & Equity chair for the Lakehead Elementary Teachers of Ontario. She was the project manager for the Urban Aboriginal Education Project and an Aboriginal Education Resource Teacher with the Lakehead Board.

Rachel is currently completing the Master of Education program at Lakehead University.

Dr. Pamela Rose Toulouse

Dr. Pamela Rose Toulouse is an associate professor in the School of Education at Laurentian University in Sudbury, Ontario. She is widely known for her research, publications, and presentations in the area of Aboriginal student self-esteem, inclusive curriculum, and Aboriginal contributions to the world.

Pamela is a proud Anishinabek woman originally from Sagamok First Nation, which is an Ojibway, Odawa, and Pottawatomi community along the north shore of Lake Huron. She began her career as an elementary school teacher on Manitoulin Island, is now a highly respected educator with over 17 years' experience at all levels, and currently works at the university level with student teachers. She has been cited in *Maclean's* magazine as one of Laurentian University's favourite professors as identified by students.

In addition to her work on the iLit series and other publications, Dr. Toulouse is set to release her groundbreaking book called *Achieving Aboriginal Student Success: A Professional Resource for K to 8 Educators*. Dr. Toulouse continues her lifelong journey and passion for education.

Series Contributors

iLit Series Education Advisors

Dr. Geraldine Balzer
University of Saskatchewan, SK

Rachel Cooke
Toronto District School Board, ON

Danielle Desjardins-Koloff
Windsor-Essex Catholic District School Board, ON

Candice Fung
Lambton Kent District School Board, ON

Starleigh Grass
Gold Trail School District 74, BC

Michael Halfin
York Region District School Board, ON

Irene Heffel
Edmonton Public School Board, AB

Lyanda Jackson
Dufferin-Peel Catholic District School Board, ON

Janet Kish
Toronto District School Board, ON

Katherine Kristalovich
Winnipeg School Division, MB

Lisa Loughlin
Toronto Catholic District School Board, ON

Dr. Janet E. McIntosh
Nipissing University, ON

Patricia S. Mountain
North Vancouver School District 44, BC

Sue Schleppe
Maple Ridge School District, BC

Ann Varty
Trillium Lakelands District School Board, ON

Alex White
Calgary District School Board, AB

Melanie White
Ottawa-Carleton District School Board, ON

Ken Whytock
Waterloo Region District School Board, ON

iLit Series Reviewers

Ashley Alexopoulos
Durham District School Board, ON

Daniel Berenstein
Toronto District School Board, ON

Ari Boublil
School District 43, BC

Cathy Coelho
Dufferin-Peel Catholic District School Board, ON

Mary Curk
Thames Valley District School Board, ON

Liza Donnelly
Regina Catholic School District, SK

Kathy Farenholtz
Langley School District, BC

Donna Giacalone-Miller
Hamilton-Wentworth Catholic District School Board, ON

Irene Heffel
Edmonton Public School Board, AB

David Helps
Waterloo Region District School Board, ON

David Koloff
Windsor-Essex Catholic District School Board, ON

Katherine Kristalovich
Winnipeg School Division 1, MB

Dr. Raymond H. Lavery
Independent Consultant, MB

Lisa Loughlin
Toronto Catholic District School Board, ON

Patricia S. Mountain
North Vancouver School District 44, BC

Siobhan Mulroy
Near North District School Board, ON

Pat Opitz
Winnipeg District School Board, MB

Natasha Salonen
Waterloo Region District School Board, ON

Sue Schleppe
Maple Ridge-Pitt Meadows 42, BC

Bryan J. Smith and Students
Thames Valley District School Board, ON

T.A. Young
St. Michaels University School, BC

About the Artists

Moses (Amik) Beaver is a First Nations artist from the fly-in reserve of Summer Beaver, Ontario (Nibinamik First Nation). His multilayered paintings are an extension of the Canadian Woodland style of art. His aim is to contribute to cultural awareness and revitalization. He works frequently with youth, both within the educational system and in community projects. His work appears in the following selections: "An Uncertain Journey on a Jagged Road" and "The Biggest Moccasins in the World."

Kristy Cameron is a Métis teacher and artist, born and raised in Atikokan, Ontario. She uses bright, dramatic colours to capture historical beliefs and legends in her paintings. When not at her canvas, she enjoys the land around Atikokan with her husband Michael, and their three daughters. Her work appears in "The Animal People Choose a Leader."

Andy Everson was born in Comox, British Columbia. He is named Nagedzi after his grandfather, Chief Andy Frank. His cultural interests lie with both his K'ómoks and Kwakwaka'wakw ancestries, and are expressed through dancing, singing, artwork, and the completion of a Master's degree in anthropology. He began taking his visual artwork more seriously in 1990, when he started designing and painting *chilkat*-style blankets for use in potlatch dancing. His work appears in "A Raven Flies South."

Jim Logan is a founding member and captain of the Métis Art Council, former co-chair of the Society of Canadian Artists of Native Ancestry (SCNA), and a recipient of the British Columbia Aboriginal Arts Award and two Canada Council Awards. He started painting what he calls his "social statement pieces" back in the early 1980s when he worked as a lay minister in Kwanlun Dunn Village on the outskirts of Whitehorse, Yukon. He now lives in Ottawa and works with the Canada Council for the Arts. Jim has three sons and two grandsons. His work appears in "My Whole Life Going Home."

Aaron Paquette descends from Cree, Cherokee, and Norwegian backgrounds. He is known for his bright colours and strong lines, and for sharing new ways of looking at age-old experiences and beliefs. Aaron is also an experienced facilitator and trainer, and an engaging public speaker. Based in Edmonton, Alberta, Aaron has been creating art for the past twenty years. His work appears in the following selections: "Mystery Girl" and "spiders."

The artwork of **Christi Belcourt**, **Chris Bose**, and **Jason EagleSpeaker** also appear in this book. You can read about these artists when you encounter their selections.

Table of Contents

Alternate Table of Contents

Reaching Goals

Social Justice, Political Struggle, and History

About Peoples Groups

The first inhabitants of North America and their descendants have specific rights within Canada. This results in the need for English words and terms that draw a distinction between different *peoples* in Canada, so that those rights can be referenced in Canadian laws. The acceptance of these terms changes over time. Here are some examples:

Aboriginal peoples: the original inhabitants of North America and their descendants. The Canadian Constitution recognizes three groups of Aboriginal people: First Nations, Métis, and Inuit.

First Peoples: a collective term for First Nations, Métis, and Inuit peoples in Canada, as well as indigenous peoples around the world

First Nations peoples: a collective term for Aboriginal peoples who are not Inuit or Métis. Many communities have also adopted the term *First Nation* to replace the word *band*. International law recognizes a *nation* as a distinct group or race of people that share history, traditions, and culture, and says that a *nation* is entitled to self-government. The term *First Nation* was adopted during the struggle by First Nations peoples to be recognized as distinct societies in Canada.

Indian: this word has a legal meaning in Canadian law and refers to Aboriginal people who are not Inuit or Métis. Many First Nations people find this term offensive and prefer to be identified more accurately by the name of their own community, (e.g., St'at'imc person, Tsilhqot'in Nation) or collectively as Aboriginal, First Nation, Native, or Indigenous people.

Métis: people of mixed First Nations and European descent who identify themselves as Métis. Some Métis people make a distinction between those who can trace their ancestry back to the Red River Valley in Manitoba, and those that can't.

Inuit: Aboriginal peoples who live in Arctic Canada, primarily in Nunavut, the Northwest Territories, and northern parts of Labrador and Quebec.

East

First Perspectives

BIG IDEA

How have your experiences defined your identity?

The sections in *Strength and Struggle* are based on the holistic wheel, which teaches us that all things are interconnected. The wheel has four directions: east, south, west, and north. According to First Nations' cultural beliefs, each direction outlines elements that are related to seasons, calendar months, race, gifts, aspects of our being, age, and personal development.

The East represents elements of spring, illumination, the physical aspects of a person, and the childhood phase of personal development.

The stories shared in this section explore perspectives of First Nations and Inuit peoples and the connection they have to the land and to others. You'll meet a young boy struggling with his father's absence and his mother's illness, a youth who overcomes overwhelming obstacles to complete high school, and a tiny, humble muskrat who risks everything to help re-create the world. The stories highlight our dedication to living our culture, despite many challenges. The poetry, graphic imagery, essays, and legends in this section shine light on the power of stories to shape our identity.

The art of storytelling is an important aspect of First Nations, Métis, and Inuit peoples' oral tradition. Stories are not something to be left in childhood. They teach us valuable lessons while entertaining and encouraging us to explore our own values, beliefs, and connection to our surroundings.

WE'RE MORE THAN JUST BEADS & FEATHERS

Graphic Novella

Written by Jason EagleSpeaker aka OHK-SIHK-IMI aka Luke WarmWater

Jason EagleSpeaker, long in name, rarer in appearance. He is a Blackfoot/Duwamish NDN born where the horizon meets earth, where the eagle and the raven fly free, under the sun and the moon (well, pretty close to there anyways) ... and raised on a strict diet of smoked salmon and buffalo jerky, pemmican and geoducks, Hostess Suzy Q's and Super Jos. Louis. Fighting ignorance since the 80s (it's taking longer than he thought), he now leads The EagleSpeaker Connection, a nonprofit organization based in Calgary, Alberta. He's also creator of the *Luke WarmWater & The Man* and *NAPI* comics, countless grassroots publications, and the residential school graphic novel *UNeducation*.

Tips

NDN: a play on the word *Indian*, used often on social networking sites, such as Facebook and Twitter, and in texting. Jason EagleSpeaker explains that "using NDN is my way of taking ownership of an otherwise misconstrued imposition on First Nations, Inuit, and Métis people (the term *Indian*) and making it a positive term of endearment."

novella: a short novel

Before

Graphic novels use both text and images to tell a story. What advantages does this format have?

During

As you read, which do you do first, read the text or view the pictures? How does one inform the other?

HOW TO APPRECIATE A GRAPHIC NOVEL

GRAPHIC NOVEL IS A TERM THAT DESCRIBES A MEDIUM, NOT A GENRE: GRAPHIC NOVELS CAN BE HISTORIES, FANTASIES, OR ANYTHING IN BETWEEN

When most people hear the phrase graphic novel they think comic books
... MAYBE EVEN SUPERHEROES COME TO MIND ...

How are graphic novels and comics books the same? ... how they're read
BOTH RELY ON PICTURES AND WORDS TO TELL THE STORY. TYPICALLY THE PICTURES ARE ARRANGED ON THE PAGE IN SEQUENTIAL PANELS, WHILE THE WORDS ARE PRESENTED IN SPEECH BUBBLES (FOR DIALOGUE) OR TEXT BOXES (FOR NARRATION).

How are graphic novels and comic books different?
GRAPHIC NOVELS DIFFER FROM COMICS IN THAT THEY USUALLY CONTAIN STAND-ALONE STORIES AND COMPLEX PLOTS.

GRAPHIC NOVELS ARE NOT COLLECTIONS OF COMIC STRIPS ...

AM EAGLESPEAKER
THE PRODUCT OF A DUWAMISH NDN
THAT SCRATCHED THE BACK ...
OF A BLACKFOOT LADY NAMED LINDA
HIS MOM'S IN THE HOSPITAL FOR JUST A BIT LONGER, SHE NAMED HIM JASON.
JASON! HE'S GONNA NEED A BLACKFOOT NAME TOO!
YOUR PEOPLE WILL KNOW YOU AS OHK-SIHK-IMI PII-TAH-POYI. THIS RED OCHRE WILL PROTECT YOU.
OHK-SIHK-IMI
OHK-SIHK-IMI
OHK SIHK IMI
OHK-SIHK-IMI
MY GRANDSON, OHK-SIHK-IMI
WE'RE MOVING BACK TO CANADA. WE WANT TO TAKE JASON.
I DON'T KNOW. HE'S A LI'L YOUNG. HOW 'BOUT IF HE SPENDS TIME HERE ON THE COAST AND BACK HOME?
... AND THAT'S HOW NAPI ROASTED GOPHERS ... OH LOOK MY BOY, WE'RE ALMOST THERE!
THE REZ
POPULATION: 10,436 NDNS
... AND 4 OR 5 BRAVE WHITE PEOPLE

I AM "THE BOY FROM TWO RESERVES"
OHK-SIHK-IMI, MAKE SURE YOU PAINT BETWEEN THOSE LINES. DON'T MAKE ME COME OVER THERE!
YOU GOT IT, GRANDMA!
PAINTING THE TIPI
DON'T LET THAT CLAM GET AWAY!
DIGGING FOR GEODUCKS
WAYLUM SKWUM CHEY --- KASHWA
THE "PADDLE TO SEATTLE"
CHECK THIS NEW MOVE OUT, I CALL IT THE "BANNOCK SLAP."
BOY'S TRADITIONAL
RIDING HORSES IS FUN, BUT I MAKE IT LOOK GOOD!
BAREBACK RIDING
THE ONE MY FAMILY WOULD CALL THAT "HALF BUFFALO, HALF SALMON NDN"
LOOK AT ME, DAD!
COLUMBIA RIVER
HOLEE, WE HAVE ENOUGH FOR THE WHOLE WINTER!
PICKIN' SASKATOONS
YOU GOT IT, EAGLESPEAKER!
POTLATCH CEREMONY

AM THE GRANDSON OF THE LATE GREAT GLEN EAGLESPEAKER
ARE YOU A LEADER OR A FOLLOWER?
I'M A LEADER !
HE SHOWED ME HUMILITY RESPECT HONESTY BRAVERY WISDOM TRUTH AND LOVE
S FAME GREW QUICKLY
ALWAYS LOOK A PERSON IN THE EYE.
GLEN EAGLESPE
LIMITED ENGAGEM
AMERICAN INDIAN
THAT WAY THEY RESPECT YOU BETTER, HEY GRANDPA?
I DEDICATE THIS PIECE TO THE CITY OF SEATTLE.

I AM FLYING ALL OVER NORTH AMERICA
ART SHOWS TAKE US CITY TO CI
LOOK GRANDPA, I CAN SEE SEATTLE FROM HERE. WE'RE ALMOST HOME!
THE BEST PART OF ANY TRIP IS 'COMING HOME'
I AM FLYING ALL OVER THE WORLD
THE CALGARY EXHIBITION & STAMPED TOUR TAKES US COUNTRY TO COUNTR

AM ABOUT TO BEGIN MY 'REAL' JOURNEY
CHECK IT OUT, MA! IT'S ANOTHER PACKAGE FROM GRANDPA --- IT'S FULL OF ---
HUH ? --- WHAT --- WHAT'S WRONG MAMA? --- WHAT'S WRONG MAMA? ---
ITS GRANDPA --- HE'S --- HE'S --- HE'S GONE SON --- HE'S GONE
NOT MY GRANDPA
NOT MY GRANDPA
NOT MY GRANDPA

I AM STARTING TO 'NOTICE' THINGS
HEY LONGHAIR, WHAT'S THE DIFFERENCE BETWEEN A PICNIC TABLE AND AN NDN? A PICNIC TABLE CAN SUPPORT A FAMILY
I AM AN NDN BOY
NO GIRLS ALLOWED
HEY ... POCAHONTAS ... WHY DON'T YOU DANCE FOR US?
NO BRAIDS
BRAIDS
I'M AN NDN BOY !!!
MY BROTHER THINKS YOU'RE CUTE
BUT, I'M AN NDN BOY ?
I'M A LITTLE NDN BOY!

AM BEGINNING TO 'UNDERSTAND' THINGS
HE GETS INTO FIGHTS EVERY DAY AND DISRUPTS THE CLASS. HE HAS SPECIAL NEEDS
DOES HE FINISH HIS WORK?
WELL ... YES ... BUT ...
TSAA ... HE'S JUST BORED ... TEST HIM!
NEVER RESPECT THOSE THAT DON'T RESPECT YOU BACK
NAPIKOAN UNIVERSIT
MASTER OF NDN STUDIES
ORIZON
NDAY, JANUARY 6, 1985
EAGLESPEAKER BROTHERS ARE FIRST EVER AMERICAN INDIAN STUDENTS ACCEPTED INTO THE GIFTED STUDENTS PROGRAM
AM 'RECOGNIZED'
I EXCEL
HOLEE ... THAT'S EASY, MR COOK! THE CUBE ROOT OF 729 IS 9
GNORANCE S BLISS ...
HAPPY HALLOWEEN
MAN ... WHAT THE HECK TRIBE ARE Y'ALL FROM?
BOYS, WE'RE MOVING TO CANADA. GRANDMA NEEDS US NOW
FOR REAL? ... THE REZ? ... CAN WE LEAVE TONIGHT?
I EMBRACE CHANGE
AM ... REZ BOUND
BLOOD TRIBE ... HERE I COME ... BLOOD TRIBE ... HERE I COME

I AM DANCING AT THE CALGARY STAMPEDE GRANDSTAND
THE CROWD IS GOING WILD, MY FRIENDS LOVE IT ... SOMETHING FEELS DIFFERENT, IT'S NOT THE SAME
I DON'T FEEL RIGHT
THEY LOVE ME ?
NDNS ARE NEAT ...
NICE OUTFIT
CUTE KID
OOH ... BEADS
OOH ... FEATHERS
THEY HATE ME
HE JUST WANTS A HANDOUT
WHERE'S YOUR COSTUME?
FUTURE DRUNK
ENTERTAIN ME, NOW!
GET A HAIRCUT
BEADS
FEATHERS
DRUNK
LONG HAIR
I'M OUTTA HERE !
... WE'RE MORE THAN JUST BEADS & FEATHERS

AM IN FRONT OF THE LINE
THE SUN'S BEEN STARING AT ME FOR HOURS
MAN, IT'S SO HOT OUT HERE, I BET YOU GET A SUNBURN AT NIGHT ...
MY FLESH OFFERINGS STING A LITTLE
I THINK ... I'M FAINTING
ARE YOU OKAY, BROTHER ?
BE WARY
ANY FOOL CAN IMPRESS STRANGERS, ONLY REAL MEN ARE LEADERS FOR THEIR FAMILY
... AND REMEMBER KIDS, YOU ARE THE FUTURE. I BELIEVE IN YOU ...
Alex Two Face
WHAT ABOUT US, DAD?
E CHARY
... I LIVE BENEATH THE MOON AND THE STARS, WHERE THE HORIZON MEETS THE EARTH, WHERE THE EAGLE AND THE RAVEN FLY FREE ...
... CULTURE PIMPS ARE EVERYWHERE
... AND ... FOR ONLY $999, YOU TOO CAN EXPERIENCE AN 'AUTHENTIC NDN' SWEATLODGE CEREMONY/GIFT SHOP ... AND IF YOU ACT NOW, I WILL THROW IN A BLESSING AND A FREE SMUDGE KIT FOR THE KIDS ...
CULTURE FOR SALE
E LEERY
... NEXT UP, INTERTRIBAL ... SOBRIETY SOCIETY ... TAKE IT AWAY ...
... THINGS ARE NOT ALWAYS WHAT THEY SEEM
GEEZ ... THERE YOU ARE! DRUM JUDGING STARTS IN 10 MINUTES ... HUH? ... AWW MAN ... WHAT'S WITH THE BLOODSHOT EYES?
WHERE'S MY SUNGLASSES?
TSAA, THIS GUY DON'T WORRY ABOUT IT ... JUST MEET US BACK AT THE DRUM ...
I'M TAPPIN' OUT, BOYS

I AM WAITING FOR THE POWER TO RUN OUT ON THE MOON
AND THAT'LL BE SOMETIME SOON
NOW LEAVIN
SCARED OF CHANGE? .. TURN BACK NOW
THE RE
THE REZ IS WHERE I'M FROM ... BUT IT'S NOT WHAT I AM ...
I AM HOMELESS
I CHERISH THE TWILIGHT
OH YESSS ... ALMOST DAYLIGHT ... I BETTA HIT THAT SOUP LINE AND GET TO SCHOOL
MY SOUL IS THE RIGHT SIZE
SEED
THE MUSTARD SEED STREET MINISTRY
GEEZ ... ITS COLDER THAN A POLAR BEAR'S TOENAIL OUT HERE!

AM AN ADULT NOW
SURE, LOTSA PEOPLE GET THEIR DIPLOMA ... BUT ... I LOOK GOOD DOING IT ...
P.I.C.S.S
PLAINS INDIAN CULTURAL SURVIVAL SCHOOL
... MY SWAGGER REMAINS INTACT
I MEAN ... "MY SWAGGER IS USUALLY INTACT"
HAHA .. YOU'RE SO FUNNY, EAGLE ... "CAMP COUNSELLOR DRESS-UP" IS ALWAYS THE BEST ...
I COMMAND RESPECT ... I NEVER DEMAND IT!
GREAT IDEAS EVERYONE. LET'S GET IT DONE TOGETHER!
INSPIRE BY EXAMPLE
YOU CAN DO IT! JUST LIKE I SHOWED YOU!
THE RICHEST ARE THOSE WHO GIVE THE MOST AWAY
HEY NDNS, FREE HERITAGE PARK TICKETS FOR THE WHOLE FAMILY!
RKING FOR OTHERS HAS ITS DRAWBACKS
AWW MAN ... WHAT THE ... ?
YET ANOTHER NDN PROGRAM
Loses Funding Over Governance Issues
I DON'T KNOW WHAT THIS WORLD IS COMING TO ..

I AM FORMULATING PLANS
I'M GONNA DO MY OWN THING, BUT I NEED A NAME FOR THESE NDN COMICS ---
IDEAS CAN COME FROM EVERYWHERE
SOMEONE'S AT THE DOOR
IT'S FROM GRANDP
GRANDPA'S STORIES ---
--- THEN NAPI'S EYEBALLS JUMPED OUT OF HIS SOCKETS AND FLEW OVER TO A FARAWAY BRANCH --- THE CHICKADEES JUST LAUGHED --- THEN ---
LOOK AT THAT BOY WITH BRAIDS --- LET'S CALL HIM LUKE WARMWATER --- LUKE WARMWATER --- LUKE WARMWATER --- LUKE WARMWATER
HOLEE --- WHAT A CLEVER NAME ---
CHILDHOOD 'TEASIN
TODAY ---
UNEDUCATION – A RESIDENTIAL SCHOOL GRAPHIC NOVEL – PART 1: --- I LEARNED ALL OF LIFE'S MOST IMPORTANT LESSONS BEFORE I WAS 10 ---
WE'RE MORE THAN JUST BEADS AND FEATHER

What Inspired Me to Write This Selection

"We're More Than Just Beads & Feathers" is based on a personal life philosophy that I've followed since I was ten. It's a graphic memoir of an NDN boy realizing hypocrisies and wanting to live beyond the stereotypes.

I choose to embrace connection by showing others how traditional NDN values are relevant in today's society. Sincere humility, respect, honesty, bravery, wisdom, truth, and love are a modern-day roadmap to success and true happiness—we all need inspiration by example. I *honour* our past, I don't *live* in it.

I choose to welcome humour because it bridges the gap between the way things are and the way things should be. In addition to our strength, resilience, passion, determination, and spirituality, we are also a hilarious and light-hearted people. Personally, I don't feel this side of us is reflected enough in educational literature.

My whole family asks each of you to look beyond the beads and feathers. You will see a burgeoning NDN community that can, does, and will master all of mainstream society's challenges.

The rez is where I'm from, but it's not what I am.

After

1. **Critical Literacy** Who do you think the author was trying to reach by choosing to tell his story using this graphic novel format?
2. **Reading for Meaning** The narrator says that his grandpa showed him "humility, respect, honesty, bravery, wisdom, truth, and love." Within the text and illustrations, find evidence for these teachings.
3. **Understanding Form and Style** There are many defining moments in this story.
   a) What graphic techniques does the author use to highlight these moments?
   b) Are these techniques effective in communicating meaning? Why or why not?
4. **Reading for Meaning** The author includes many details in the background of his illustrations. Reread the story and look for these details. What messages are these details conveying?
5. **Metacognition** Were there any moments in the story where you were confused? If so, what strategies did you use to resolve this confusion?
6. **Reading for Meaning**
   a) As the author grows up, he encounters many different messages about himself and his culture. Identify these messages and who they came from.
   b) How does the author use these conflicting messages to make sense of his identity?

Beyond

Student Voice Create a graphic panel, or other visual representation, illustrating an event in your life that relates in some way to this story. Explain the relationship between this event and the author's story.

Footprints in the Snow

Poetry

Written by Nichola Batzel

Nichola Batzel was born in Churchill, Manitoba, to an Inuit mother and an English-Norwegian father, and was adopted into the Batzel family. She identifies with her given name, her spirit name of *Wabishki Mahkwa Equay* given to her by an Anishinaabe elder, and her Inuit name of *Tookoome*. All play a role in how she views her role as an educator, a mother, and a member of her family and community.

Tips

ajaaja: a traditional Inuit song, often involving stories about people and their travels

Wabishki Mahkwa Equay: white bear woman [in the Ojibway language]

N'dizhinigaaz: my name is [in the Ojibway language]

Uvunga: my name is [in the Inuktitut language]

Tookoome: the poet's Inuit name

stanza: a grouping of lines in a poem, set off by a space

Before

Brainstorm what you know about Inuit life and culture.

During

As you read, visualize what the poet is describing. What words and phrases helped you visualize?

Have you heard the crunch in the snow as you travel
on your journey?
Have you taken time to look at the footprints
you leave behind?

As I walk and leave footprints in the snow,
My son follows and jumps in the impressions
I leave behind.

What does he see? What does he learn
From my footprints in the snow?

I am the white bear from the Great White North,
Who walks among the trees and the West wind
of the South.

I walk with relatives but often not side by side with fellow bears;
My fellow bears who live in the land of caribou, ice and snow.

My stride is longer and paws bigger than those found here.
My fur made to withstand the icy cold and the Northern winds.

Has the rhythm of my stride harmonized to a new and extraneous land?
As the rhythm of my ancestors' *ajaajas* and drum dancing is not heard here.

How do I blend to those whose songs run deep within this land?
And yet remember my original song of the bears from the land of caribou,
ice and snow?
"*Wabishki Mahkwa Equay N'dizhinigaaz*" is what the Inuit woman says ...
Followed by "*Uvunga Tookoome*."

I walk and leave footprints in the snow.
As I grow older I realize I must be aware of what I leave behind.

Proud to acknowledge who I am,
Yet flexible enough to adjust to the songs of others.

I attempt to walk with peace and balance within my stride
As my son picks up what I leave behind.

I hope he learns to harmonize with the rhythm of his song
As he dances in the snow.

Stop and embrace the rhythm of your steps
As we all dance together and leave footprints in the snow.

What Inspired Me to Write This Selection

"Being able to portray the North, with its bounty of life and beauty, to someone who has never been there is a joy. An Inuit elder once said to me that all life should be seen with beauty. When I become caught up in the hustle and bustle of life, I take a moment to remember that. This is the beauty I hope to convey in poems such as the one shared here."

After

1. **Reading for Meaning** Choose one of the following relationships and explain how the poet portrays this relationship in this poem: mother/son, person/land, present/future/past, or home/away.
2. **Critical Literacy** How do you think the poet views the people from "the South" as opposed to people from the "Great White North . . . the land of caribou, ice and snow"? What makes you think this?
3. **Reading for Meaning** After reading this poem, how have your views and assumptions about Inuit culture changed or been affirmed?
4. **Understanding Form and Style** Identify the elements of poetry used in this text. What makes their use effective?
5. **Student Voice** How would you answer the two questions that the poet poses at the beginning of this poem?
6. **Metacognition** How did visualizing help you understand the poem?

Beyond

Reading for Meaning Choose a stanza you consider to be very visual. Why did this stanza stand out for you? Create a visual representation of this stanza, and include an explanation of its significance.

A Raven Flies South

Short Story

Written by Gord Bruyere

Gord Bruyere is Anishnabe and originally from Couchiching First Nation in northwestern Ontario. He is a writer, teacher, program/curriculum developer, and researcher. He has published a book, poetry, and journal articles that focus on Aboriginal issues in education, child welfare, traditional Anishnabe family beliefs, and antiracism. He currently lives in Lakefield, Ontario.

Tips

tobacco: a traditional medicine that is offered as a gift to the earth or elder

***kookum*:** grandma [in the Oji-Cree or Cree languages]; In this story, Raven calls his grandma "Kooks" which is short for *kookum*.

Before

As you get older, do you find you have more responsibility? What kinds of responsibilities do you have? How do you feel about these responsibilities?

During

As you read this story, think about questions that you would like to ask the author.

A raven flies south across the face of the full November moon. Colony Farm is still purple before dawn but the frost on the brown grasses and bare trees is already visible. Above them, the sky is shifting layers from the black horizon of the Coquitlam hills, through the mix of magentas where the moon lies, to the upper blue that assures the return of the sun. The raven circles back. Its dipped wing touches the mountains far away. Snow will soon find its way down to the valleys. A white sheen across the abandoned farmland sliced by a winter-shallow river promises that.

His name is Raven too. He is one of those children who wakes without being told. In fact, he is usually up before anyone else in the house. Like his namesake, the morning thrills him. It is special to be the only one awake. He cautiously pours cereal and milk in hopes it won't give him away, tiptoes to avoid the squeaky spots on the tiled floor, and slips outside. Raven, the boy, always feels a bit rushed and tense, but only because he wants to hold onto the feeling that comes from being the only one around. It feels like the world belongs to him.

The birds are still hidden in the trees, except for that raven. Their sleepy voices are soft as if trying to protect his alone time. They will have other voices to feed, just like he will soon. He will have to go back inside soon. He sighs and pauses, then takes a deep breath and begins to walk. The frozen grasses down to the river look like dead spider legs, only white. Grandma says, "There are people like us who believe spider was the first woman." "Mom is the first woman to me," Raven smiles to himself, "and Kooks is next." Sometimes it's the other way around.

He sighs again and turns back down the hill. It is already brighter. The sun now touches the mountains and turns the peaks pink. The moon has bedtime soon. The frost is turning into mist following the river and swimming across the valley like a water snake or a salmon in the shallows.

He picks his way down to the river. He likes to leave no trail if he can. He hops and big-steps from a bunch of grass to a rock to a patch of bare ground. He has to do it fast so it is harder to do. Sometimes he pretends he is being chased by spies. The frost has already moistened on these spots and hides his trail. Today is even better because

Confessions to the Moon by Andy Everson

he can step onto frozen puddles and hear the crunch and crash. It leaves a print and the proof of muddy water, but he likes the sound. He must remember to clean his boots off before he goes back inside.

His path leads to the edge of the slow-moving river. It is sleepy too and that makes him feel more awake than the river, at least for a little while. That makes him feel strong. He balls his fists in front of his belly and tenses his muscles. He knows his arms are skinny and he is being crazy, and he laughs. He remembers why he is here.

Grandma said, "You have to approach these times like a warrior with serious intent." He had nodded at the time but didn't really understand. He doesn't like fighting and the only tent he had was the saggy orange pup tent rotting in the backyard. That doesn't make any sense. He knows the word *serious* though. He stands there and remembers what she had told him: "Our people used to begin every day like this and it's what made us strong." Not like these days. He wants to be strong and his arms aren't very big at all, not like those wrestlers his uncles watch, so he thinks it's a good idea to do what the old lady said.

"We put an offering in the water and pray, and we don't pray like Christians either," she said.

His Mom was a Christian and what's wrong with that, he wonders. Maybe that had something to do with why she was sad all the time. Oh yeah, Grandma. Our people don't ask for things and we are never afraid when we pray. All we do is be thankful. "Put tobacco in the water, my boy," the old woman said, "and with all your heart say thank you. If you do it right, the tobacco will warm in your hand and the water will lap at your feet." He didn't believe her about that at first, but she is right. He isn't sure if using cereal is as good as tobacco but he didn't want to steal any of Mom's cigarettes. He takes the handful of cereal out of his pocket, extends his arm out over the water and closes his eyes. Sometimes it is hard to make the feeling come. Sometimes the feeling in his stomach is too strong. Not today. Today it is easy and, with closed eyes, and with skinny arm held out, he slowly sprinkles crushed Cheerios into the Coquitlam River.

Raven, the boy, looks around. Ooh, it's like I'm inside that snake or salmon made of this mist, he thinks. "You are a salmon too because you are a twin," his grandma had told him. His brother was gone now. Mom said Jesus took him home. "No, my little man," Kooks said. He calls his grandma Kooks when he talks to her because she likes that. "Jesus didn't have that power," she said. "He was a good man and you could learn from how he lived. But we have always known that Creator makes everything including death." A third sigh.

Jesus was a fisherman. Kooks made Mom laugh when she said that was the only thing Dad and Jesus had in common. The men who fish would be up early like him.

"A good man gets up before the sun," Kooks said. Raven doesn't know what time Dad gets up. The river wanders away to go find out for him.

It's time to go back inside. He will line up the cereal boxes, place a bowl and spoon on each side of the table so those brats won't fight, take out the milk again, and go wake everyone up. He has to get the school clothes out and get lunches. He has to find the key on a shoelace that Dolly was twirling around last night and remember to put it around his neck to keep safe. He can't get mad at them because it will only get everyone upset. He has to be kind and grown up. There is a lot to remember and Raven starts to get that feeling in his stomach again.

"Only until Mom gets better," Kooks said. The sun is up now. The moon is asleep. Now where did that raven go?

One last sigh and he turns to open the door.

What Inspired Me to Write This Selection

"I woke before dawn and witnessed what I wrote as the first line of the story. I caught the story through my window and held it long enough to write it down pretty much as it appears in this anthology. Or it caught me. Either way, I'm grateful to share it and so is Raven."

After

1. **Understanding Form and Style** How does the author use imagery to convey Raven's love for his surroundings?
2. **Reading for Meaning** What evidence can you find in the story about the emotional state of Raven's mother? How does this affect Raven?
3. **Reading for Meaning** Why do you think Raven performs the ceremony by the river?
4. **Critical Literacy** Why do you think the mother's voice is not heard in this story?
5. **Student Voice** Are there any similarities between you and the character in the story? Explain.
6. **Metacognition** What strategies did you use to help you understand the story?

Beyond

Reading for Meaning Draw the outline of a head. Inside the head, draw any symbols, words, or images that are in Raven's mind in this story. Explain your drawing orally or in writing.

An Uncertain Journey on a Jagged Road

Personal Account

Originally published by SEVEN Youth Media

Written by Forrest Rain Shapwaykeesic

Forrest Rain Shapwaykeesic is from Eabematoong First Nation (Fort Hope), in northern Ontario. He loves to learn new things, work with Photoshop, tell jokes, play games, and use the Internet. He lives in Thunder Bay, Ontario, and is currently getting ready for college.

Before

Reflect on the title and predict the themes, issues, and conflicts you believe will be presented in this selection.

During

As you read the personal account, note the key challenges that the author faced in his journey from childhood to adulthood. Use a graphic organizer to record these challenges.

My name is Forrest Rain Shapwaykeesic. This story is about my journey to get my high school diploma.

I grew up in Thunder Bay, Ontario. Our family moved all the time, from house to house, school to school. Although my mother quit drinking when we were young, our home life was still not a simple one. I am the youngest sibling with three older sisters.

When I failed Grade 1, I was told I had a learning disability. And since then, I've struggled through school. Words like *dumb* and *stupid* were part of a daily vocabulary for me. By Grade 9, they diagnosed me with dyslexia. In order to read books, I had to place a purple film over the pages to see the words properly.

When I was in high school, my mother worked out of town. My youngest sister and I had the task of raising our young nephew. We were alone most of the time and we fought often in those days, sometimes even over food. During these trying times, I turned to drugs and alcohol to deal with the pain I felt in my life. When the anger was too great, I learned that self-mutilation would often relieve the hurtful feelings inside me. This became my coping method, which then became another addiction. Again I changed schools when my mother moved my nephew and me to Grand Portage, Minnesota.

Things didn't improve and at one point I was admitted to a mental hospital in Duluth for trying to hurt myself during a drinking binge. After a few days, I was released.

It wasn't long before I moved yet again. I moved back to Thunder Bay to live with a sister, then with a friend, and even in Sioux Lookout for a while. At the beginning of the next semester, I went to live with my oldest sister in Dryden to help with the kids. I was in Grade 11 by this time and was being funded by my First Nation to go to school.

Reach for Your Dreams by Moses (Amik) Beaver

My studies continued to frustrate me. Grade 11 math was hard and I couldn't keep up with the rest of the class. Soon I was skipping classes, then eventually I just stopped going.

In the first semester, the funding I was getting from my First Nation to pay for room and board was cut off. In the new year, I found a job working as a gas station attendant. Later I was kicked out of the house and found myself looking for a place to live in the middle of winter. I eventually rented a house with two friends. We agreed to split the bills. In order to pay for my part, I quit school and started working full time at the gas station.

As the years passed, I continued to move around. When I left Dryden, I had to leave all of my possessions behind. I moved to Duluth, Minnesota, and worked at Fond-Du-Luth Casino. During this time, I continued to drink and do drugs. Although I still struggled with money, I had a job and made some good friends.

Then suddenly after two-and-a-half years, I was let go at work and couldn't pay my rent. Without my high school diploma, the only job I could hope for was working at a fast-food restaurant. Even then I couldn't find a job.

Since I had nowhere else to turn, my youngest sister said she'd let me live with her in a bachelor apartment back in Thunder Bay. I took all I could carry in a small two-door car.

When I went back to Thunder Bay, I began to learn about being positive and to feel good about myself. I realized that I needed to set some real goals for myself. One of my goals was to get my Grade 12 diploma. I stopped excessive drinking and quit drugs. With the support of my sister and the clarity to chase a dream, I started to attend Lakehead Adult Education Centre, which offers programming for those who wish to finish their high school diploma outside the regular high school system.

Surrounded by positive supporters and with the help of the people around me, I found the challenges of school were obstacles I could overcome. I spent hours working on homework at the apartment, and when nobody was around to help with a question, I looked on YouTube for answers with math.

During this time I joined a gym and started working out. I ate better and started to feel better. There were other activities, such as softball, that I participated in. When there was paying work, I'd do different jobs and began learning different trades. My hobbies then included learning Photoshop and doing all kinds of photo manipulations.

As I let go of the past, I began to live in the present and plan for the future. I stopped hurting myself completely.

Six months after returning to my hometown, I completed the final credits for my high school diploma. On December 18, 2009, I became a high school graduate at the age of twenty-seven. I made it to my goal.

I'm now setting new goals. With my own apartment, I'm building up my life again. College, career, travel, and family are all the things I look forward to in my life. Now that I made it to the first goal, I know I can make them all.

After

1. **Critical Literacy** Why do you think the author wrote this personal account? What impact do you think he wants to have on the people who read it?
2. **Understanding Form and Style** What kind of language is used in this selection? How does the author's writing style affect the impact of his words?
3. **Reading for Meaning** Why do you think the author changed his perspective on life when he returned to Thunder Bay?
4. **Student Voice** Can you relate to any of the challenges that the author faced in his life? Explain.
5. **Metacognition** How did thinking about your own experiences help you understand this selection?

Beyond

Student Voice Using an appropriate software program, create a page that captures the educational, personal, and social goals you have in life. Use text, images, quotes, or icons to express your goals.

Lessons from the Re-Creation Story

Essay

Written by Deborah McGregor

Deborah McGregor, PhD, is Associate Professor in the Department of Geography and Aboriginal Studies at the University of Toronto. She is Anishnaabe from Whitefish River First Nation, Birch Island, Ontario. For over two decades she has been an educator at both the university and community levels, and has been involved in curriculum development, research, and teaching. A major focus of her work has been ensuring the appropriate consideration of Aboriginal peoples' knowledge, values, and rights in environmental and resource management in Canada.

Tips

Anishnaabe: (also spelled Anishinaabe, Anishinabe, and Anishnabe depending on the community, or Anishinabek/Anishinabeg in the plural form) one of the largest First Nations groups in North America; also called Ojibway in Canada or Chippewa in the United States. Roughly translated into English, it means *the people*.

***Kitchi-Manitou*:** the Creator in Ojibway tradition

Before

Briefly relate a creation account that you have heard.

During

As you read this essay, note any similarities or differences between this Anishnaabe creation account and creation accounts that you've heard before.

Every culture has a story about how we came to be in the world. It helps explain how people relate to each other and the natural world around them. Many cultures also have a story about events that prompted a new beginning. Indigenous peoples often refer to these stories as Origin or Creation stories. We hear these stories as children. Later in life, as we enter different stages of our lives, the stories take on more meaning. The stories help define who we are as Indigenous peoples. The stories help give direction and meaning in our lives, and explain our place in the world and our relationships to others. We spend a lifetime continually learning about our proper place in the world.

The Anishnaabe stories of Creation and Re-Creation can be used to understand Anishnaabe perspectives on the environment. The stories inform us of our beginnings and provide an understanding of our relationships and responsibilities with respect to all beings of Creation. These stories have different versions that vary with the storyteller or with local cultural traditions. In the Anishnaabe Creation story, *Kitchi-Manitou* (the Creator) had a vision, and through the vision he was able to bring Creation into being. *Kitchi-Manitou* was able to envision what was possible, and bring it to life. Ever since, the Anishnaabe people have honoured this original vision, and have themselves remained visionary and creative.

The Anishnaabe Re-Creation story reinforces the original principles of harmony and respect from the Creation story, and goes further to convey fundamental ecological principles. In the version told by Anishnaabe storyteller Basil Johnston, there has been a great flood and most life on Earth has perished, with the exception of birds and water creatures. Sky-Woman (the original human) also survives and comes to rest on the back of a great turtle. She asks the water creatures to bring her soil from the bottom of the waters, so that she may use it to make new land. Here is an excerpt from Basil Johnston's account:

> Gladly, all the animals tried to serve the spirit woman. The beaver was the first to plunge into the depths. He soon surfaced out of breath and without the precious soil. The fisher tried, but he too failed. The marten went down, came up empty handed, reporting that the water was too deep. The loon tried. Although he remained out of sight for a long time, he too emerged, gasping for air. He said that it was too dark. All tried to fulfil the spirit woman's request. All failed. All were ashamed.
>
> Finally, the least of the water creatures, the muskrat, volunteered to dive. At this announcement the other water creatures laughed in scorn, because they doubted this little creature's strength and endurance. Had not they, who were strong and able, been unable to grasp soil from the bottom of the sea? How could he, muskrat, the most humble among them, succeed when they could not?
>
> Nevertheless, the little muskrat volunteered to dive. Undaunted, he disappeared into the waves. The onlookers smiled. They waited for the muskrat to emerge as empty handed as they had done. Time passed. Smiles turned to worried frowns. The small hope that each had nurtured for the success of the muskrat turned into despair. When the waiting creatures had given up, the muskrat floated to the surface more dead than alive, but he clutched in his paws a small morsel of soil. Where the great had failed, the small succeeded. (Johnston in *Ojibway Heritage*, 1976, p. 14)

The muskrat succeeds. While in some versions of the Re-Creation story he dies, in others he is revived. There are many values and lessons to be learned from this story, but one of the most compelling is that all of Creation is important; all must be respected.

If we lose or disrespect even the tiniest and seemingly most insignificant being, our own survival becomes threatened. So it is not for us to judge the merits of another; it is instead important for us to respect and honour all beings and creatures of Creation. Muskrat teaches us about ethical conduct, the actions necessary to ensure that Creation continues. Muskrat informs us about our relationships with each other and with the natural world, including teachings about co-operation, respect, honour, humility, bravery, love, and sacrifice. The Re-Creation story is fundamentally about relationships drawn from these values and shared in our stories. The idea that "everything is connected to everything else" is now recognized as a fundamental tenet of current western views on the environment. This is an ancient principle to the Anishnaabe people.

In the Creation and Re-Creation stories, instructions are given by the Creator on how to relate appropriately with all creatures. In the Anishnaabe worldview, such knowledge comes from many sources, including Creation itself. If we observe how animals and plants survive, they will help us understand how we should live. Traditionally, the Anishnaabe understood their relationship with Creation and assumed the responsibilities given to them by the Creator. For thousands of years, through successive generations, Anishnaabe children learned from their elders how to maintain and enhance their relationship with Creation. The responsibilities that one assumed were part of ensuring the continuation of Creation—what academics, scientists, and environmentalists might today call environmental ethics.

These ethics and responsibilities necessary for the continuation of Creation are embodied in the Anishnaabe concept of *Minobimaatisiiwin*. Our worldview encompasses the idea of us being co-creators, of transforming ourselves and re-creating ourselves as needed in order to meet our challenges. *Minobimaatisiiwin* emphasizes the notion of rebirth and our goal to strive for a good life. Anishnaabe environmental activist Winona LaDuke states that we must *live Minobimaatisiiwin*, not just study it, in order to maintain the cycle of sustainability and ensure our future.

After

1. **Understanding Form and Style**
   a) Whom do you think the author is speaking to in this essay? What words and phrases from the essay make you think that?
   b) What impact does the writer's language have on the selection?
2. **Critical Literacy** In the excerpt from Basil Johnston's telling of the Re-Creation story, the perspectives of the animals who failed to retrieve soil are presented.
   a) Whose perspectives are missing?
   b) Select one character's perspective that is missing, and describe briefly what that character might say or think.
3. **Reading for Meaning** The author says, "If we observe how animals and plants survive, they will help us understand how we should live." In your own words, describe what message the author is conveying.
4. **Student Voice**
   a) In your own words, explain what the author means by *environmental ethics*.
   b) Do you apply environmental ethics in your own life? If so, how? If not, explain why not.
5. **Reading for Meaning** What does the author believe is the *most important* teaching that we should receive from the Anishnaabe Re-Creation story? Choose the best answer from the choices below.
   A. All creation must be respected.
   B. Do not give up hope.
   C. Put others' needs before your own.
   D. Do not judge people by their size and looks.
6. **Metacognition**
   a) Did you find this essay easy or challenging to read? Explain why.
   b) What strategies did you use to make sense of the text?

Beyond

Reading for Meaning Research creation accounts from other cultures. Retell one creation account in a form of your choice (such as a written story, drama, or artwork) and explain the key teaching from the story.

South

Sharing Our Gifts

BIG IDEA

How do your gifts make a difference in the world?

The South represents elements of summer, innocence, the emotional aspects of a person, and the youth phase of personal development.

In this section, First Nations, Inuit, and Métis peoples share their stories, lyrics, and images that highlight the gifts that they and others possess. You will meet several women looking to their mothers and grandmothers with pride. You will laugh with a niece and her account of her unusual gift, and get a recipe for success (and a great meal) from an accomplished chef.

The stories and words in this section will inspire you. They will make you think about the struggles we all face and the strength we all possess. The writers offer insight into their identities and how they confronted issues of racism and homophobia. The words of the First Nations, Inuit, and Métis peoples, and the gifts they share will have you thinking about your own.

Walk to Morning

Speech

Written by Joseph Boyden

Joseph Boyden's first novel, *Three Day Road*, has been translated into fifteen languages. As a national and international bestseller, the novel has won the Rogers Writers' Trust Prize, the McNally Robinson Aboriginal Book of the Year Award, France's Prix Literaire, and many other awards. *Through Black Spruce*, his second novel, won the Scotiabank Giller Prize in 2008, as well as the Libris Book of the Year award. He was awarded an honorary doctorate from Nipissing University in 2009. Joseph describes himself in this way: "It seems I'm a bit of a split personality, a combination of my father and my uncle Erl. I have my father's responsibility and my uncle's belief that the world is to be travelled. I split my life between the Gulf of Mexico [New Orleans, United States] and the gulf of the Arctic [James Bay coast, Ontario]. I write and I teach writing. My heart is part Irish, part Ojibway. I'm a Canadian in America. I'm grounded by history, and I am inspired by legend. I'm part my father, part my uncle. I am a father to my son, Jacob, and I am a writer."

Before

What issues do young people face today?

During

Make note of the issues that appear in this selection and which you identified before you read it.

The first time I died was on October 31, 1982, at 11:37 PM.

Halloween. My birthday night. I was sixteen. I'd been to a party but left at its peak with the girl I was dating in order to walk her home. We were dressed as punk rockers. I wanted to be a real one but that would take another year of learning and sometimes living on the streets.

I remember the night was cold. I shivered in my leather jacket. The girl I was dating had had some drinks and I thought she was acting more drunk than she really was, saying nonsensical things and being mean to me. I was head over heels for this girl, even though some of my friends said she didn't deserve me.

Didn't deserve me. Ha. I thought I was the one who didn't deserve. Anything. For over a year I'd been wandering through a place that I didn't know how to describe and didn't realize was certainly not normal. Whatever normal is to a young teen. The pain I felt pulse through me had become so intense that in the last year I'd taken to cutting my arms open with knives to try to release it.

When we made it to my girlfriend's front door, I leaned toward her and tried to kiss her. She turned her head away, and in a suddenly sober and serious tone told me she was breaking up with me. Then she walked inside.

I remember this: the streetlights above me in this absurdly quiet residential neighbourhood seeming so white, like a row of tidal moons; the air not feeling cold anymore even though my nose ran with snot; being pulled toward the noise of a car speeding by on the wider four-lane avenue a few streets away, and that strange realization that I was walking away from home, not toward it, not a single person in sight.

I felt like I was floating, even as I felt I was going under. I'd made a firm decision for once, and just below that I knew I was no longer in control.

And then I was standing on the curb, staring out at the four-lane road, the taillights of a couple of passing cars leaving a red trail in my eyes, the headlights of one approaching. I timed it as best I could, timed it so that there was no way the car could stop or swerve. And as the headlights of that car loomed up and swallowed me, I dove. I threw myself in front of it. And in that millisecond before I hit concrete and the car crushed me, I realized that this had nothing to do with some girl or some breakup. All I knew was that I'd just become too scared to live.

This is all of the night that I recall.

Later, I was told this: that when the paramedics arrived they found me lodged under the car of an older woman who was near hysteria. Her front right wheel had run over my chest but my leather jacket had snagged on the undercarriage, preventing the rear right tire from further crushing me. As I was transported to the hospital, my heart stopped and all vital signs were lost a number of times. My first death became many little ones.

Emergency surgery found too many injuries to list now, but here are a few: major head trauma, lacerated liver and spleen, collapsed and punctured lungs, massive internal bleeding, a splintered rib cage. And yet, for some reason no doctor at the scene dared imagine, I survived.

I do have a body littered with reminders, again too many to list, but here are a few: a thick and angry red jagged line running from my upper sternum to my groin, numerous large white scars on my skull. And the strangest—a literal tire track that runs the left side of my back.

* * *

Before you begin to think that I am the least bit proud of any of it, please hear this: until today, only my immediate family and a handful of friends knew this story.

I decided to tell this story to you, a stranger, because of a small, mostly First Nations community hundreds of kilometres north of Toronto, a place dear to my heart, a place where I lived. This place continues to drive my writing imagination; it's a town of maybe 2500 souls, and it's where eight young Indian people have taken their lives in the last number of months. A few of them are children of friends of mine.

And despite First Nations children taking their own lives in far greater numbers than other youth in this country, or on this globe, this is not a story only about our Native children. This is a story about unbearable pain that crosses race and age and gender, pain that none of us wishes to talk about. But we have to. This is about all of our children. This is about us.

Here's what I need to say to those who might be in the place I once was: I made a great mistake in attempting to do what I did. I was very, very wrong. The act is wrong. Not because of some belief that you will burn in hell. What happens when you are gone happens when you are gone. It's what happens to the ones who are left. The people who

you love, and who love you. They are ruined for the rest of their lives. There is never any real healing, just a horrible jagged and inflamed scar that marks the damage.

* * *

But I'm not telling you this most intimate mistake of my life in order to lecture. I do think about it once in a while still, and even though it occurred so long ago, it never feels very far away. I sometimes catch myself thinking, what if I'd managed it? What if I'd died? Just look at what I would have missed.

And it isn't even the big stuff, the grand stuff that comes to mind. It's always the little moments that catch me off guard. The weight of my wife's foot on my own under the covers at night. The puppy smell of our new dog. Feeling the tug on my fishing rod when the pickerel strikes my lure. Arguing with my teenage son about finding a job. It's these moments that make me thankful for my failure that night of my sixteenth birthday. That's when I give deep thanks that I failed.

* * *

I tell this story in the hope of reaching someone out there, even one person who is suffering the pain I speak of. If you hear this, talk. Speak it out loud. Walk through that night if you need to, walk away from the road. Walk to morning. Allow this pain to be exposed to sunlight instead.

After

1. **Metacognition** What types of questions did you ask yourself as you were reading the selection?
2. **Reading for Meaning**
   a) What message is the author trying to convey in this selection?
   b) Do you think he is successful? Explain why or why not.
3. **Student Voice** The author says, "What if I'd died? Just look at what I would have missed."
   a) What things does he say he is thankful that he didn't miss?
   b) Do the things he identifies surprise you? How do you relate to these things?
4. **Critical Literacy** This selection was originally a speech given to a group of high school students in Bracebridge, Ontario. Do you think the language, tone, and content are appropriate for this audience? Explain why or why not.
5. **Understanding Form and Style** Identify elements of language in this selection that make it sound like a speech.

Beyond

Creating Media Texts Research services in your area that help youth in crisis. Create a plan to advertise these services to the students in your school and/or community. Carry out your plan.

I Am My Grandmother

Graphic Journal

Written by Nadia McLaren

Nadia McLaren was born in northern Quebec and raised in small communities across northwestern Ontario. She attended the Ontario College of Art and Design, graduating in 2003—the same year her grandmother passed away. She set out to honour the memory of her grandparents, all elders, and residential school survivors through her award-winning documentary, *Muffins for Granny*. Nadia lives in Toronto, Ontario, with her husband, Fabio Sartori, and young son, Leo.

Tips

residential schools: boarding schools run from mainly the 1830s to the 1950s to educate First Nations, Métis, and Inuit children and erase their traditional languages and cultures. Students were often forcibly removed from their homes and families and subjected to abuse in these schools. The last federally-run residential school closed in 1996 in Saskatchewan.

simile: a comparison made using the words *like* or *as*

Before

Glance over the images and predict what the text is about.

During

As you read, think about how the title connects to the rest of the selection.

"I am my Grandmother"

I am my grandmother.

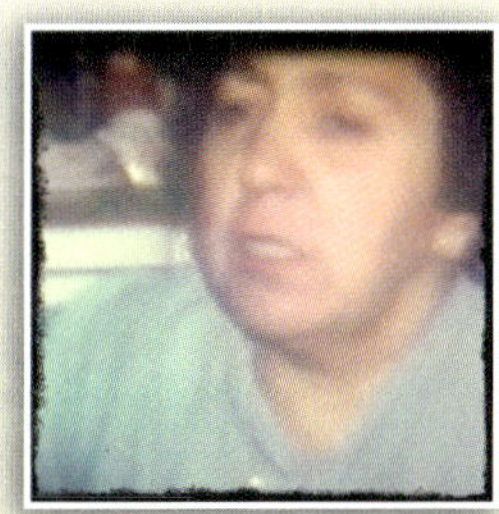

All her words, laughter, and tears are inside me forever.

This is my Granny.

When I close my eyes, these are the pictures I see—this is the way I remember and cherish her.

Granny was an Ojibway from a place on the north shore of the great Lake Superior called Heron Bay, Pic River reservation.

She was my greatest gift.

I am one of many grandchildren and I wonder if my cousins feel it too—

The “restlessness of an ancient sadness.”

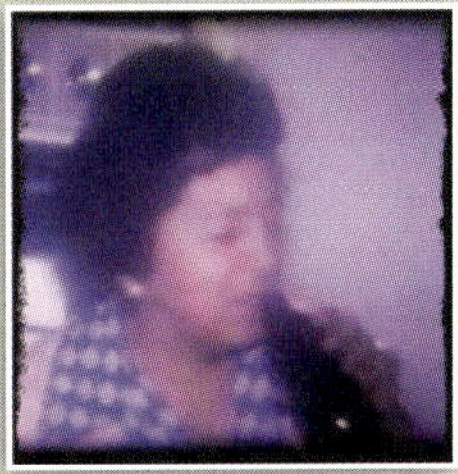

I am reminded of days when I could barely see over the kitchen table she sat at. When I stared beyond the bottles of booze and watched her cry.

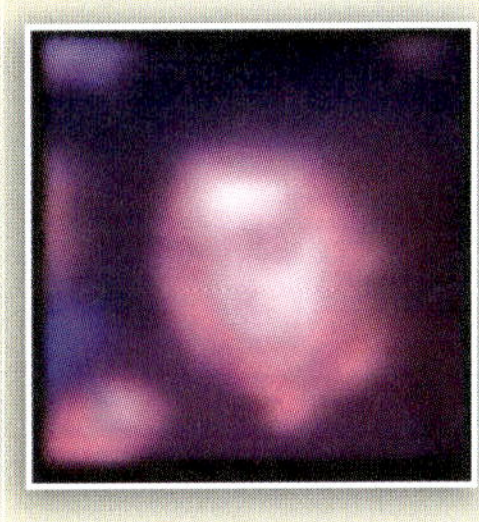

She spoke of her childhood and she said her mother died when she was four. She spoke of a place called residential school where she was abused in ways I can’t bear to imagine.

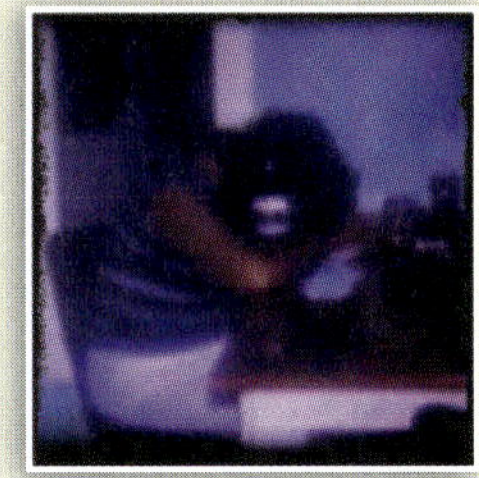

Then, she never spoke of it again.

This land, my home, has spoken.

Like the wind, it speaks of a storm brewing in places that have remained quiet for far too long—places not far from here.

The wind has called me back within the trees to once again breathe inside an atmosphere that feels like the very lungs of Mother Earth.

There are many ghosts that whisper.

And like the cool, sticky air, they have penetrated my skin and sit just beneath the surface.

I wonder how long the
ghosts will stay with me.

And sometimes I wonder
if holding onto the
memories is holding
me back.

It is difficult to explain
how my skin remembers
something that hasn't
happened yet.

The familiar awaits me and
this journey longs to leave
the unfamiliar behind.

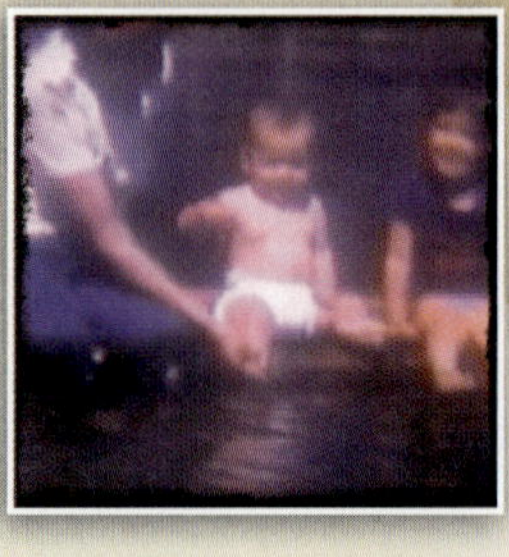

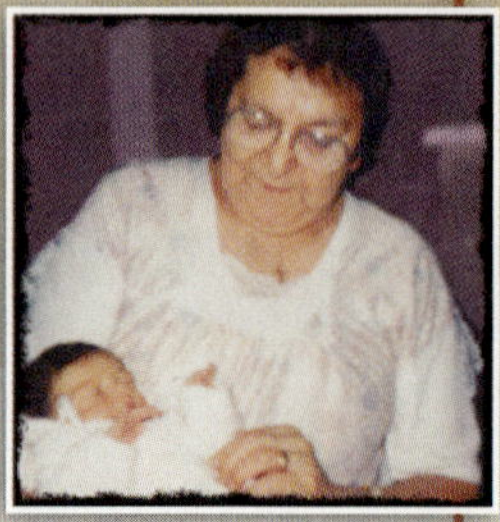

I am my grandmother.

Granny was an Ojibway from a place called Heron Bay, Pic River Reservation. She was my greatest gift.

Everything she was began there, and everything she became in all her loving, her strength, and beauty now dawns the mornings of the places we can look forward to. Some might call it Heaven ... but for many, that place is simply called Hope.

Theresa McCraw
... all her words, laughter, and tears ... are Love.

What Inspired Me to Write This Selection

"This piece is my personal reflection based on the film I wrote, directed, and produced called *Muffins for Granny*. When my Granny passed away, I felt that a huge part of me had gone with her. The documentary journey was a way of coping with the grief and loss I felt at the time. My peace was found in the very last interview I conducted for the documentary. A Métis woman named Carrielynn Lamouche said, "What you need to realize is that when you breathe, it is your grandmother that is breathing through you. And when you speak, she will be speaking through you." Carrielynn also said, "The grandmothers teach us that a gentle voice is much more powerful than any enraged warrior."

I have come to realize how important it is to tell these stories, Granny's story and my story. And I have grown to know that "your truth is your beauty. And your story is your gift." Meegwetch."

After

1. **Metacognition** Was the prediction you made in the Before reading question confirmed when you read the text? Explain what strategies you used to confirm your prediction.
2. **Understanding Form and Style** Give an example of a simile that the author has used in this selection. How does the simile impact the author's description of her experience?
3. **Reading for Meaning** What do you think the author means by "the restlessness of an ancient sadness"?
4. **Understanding Form and Style** How effective is the use of the photographs in conveying the author's connection and appreciation for her grandmother? Give an example of a photograph from this selection that supports the author's message.
5. **Critical Literacy** How do you think the grandmother would feel reading the author's journal? What words in the text make you think so?
6. **Student Voice** How did reading this selection make you feel? Explain.

Beyond

Listening and Speaking Imagine you are a talk show host. Who would you invite to be your guest—the author or the grandmother? Write two or three questions you would like to ask. Work with a partner and answer each other's questions based on what you have learned in this selection. Together write a script, including questions and answers, for the talk show or dramatize the talk show for the class.

E5-770, My Mother's Name

Song Lyrics

Written by Lucie Idlout

Lucie Idlout is of Inuit heritage and has lived much of her early life in the High Arctic on North Baffin Island, Northwest Territories, now Nunavut. Her passion as a songwriter and artist stretches far beyond the treeline, since she has also lived in several southern Canadian cities. In recent years, she has split her time between Toronto, Ontario, and Iqaluit, Nunavut.

Tip

metaphor: a comparison of two items not usually seen as similar, but without using the words *like* or *as*. In this song, the writer uses *cattled* and *farmed* to compare the treatment of her mother to the treatment of cattle.

Before

In what ways are people identified by numbers? What numbering systems are used to identify you? Use a graphic organizer to sort your ideas into categories.

During

E5-770 is part of an identification system for Inuit introduced by the government of Canada in 1941. The government imposed this number system on Inuit so they could be tracked, especially for tuberculosis cases. The government felt this was more efficient than trying to standardize name spellings. The giving of names is very important in Inuit society, and to not have these names recognized by the government can be viewed as a way to dehumanize the Inuit and take away their identity. Think about this background information as you read the poem.

Your tongue unfit, too frail to speak
Identities of thousands cattled 'E'
E5-770, my mother's name.

Had you ever wondered of the days to face you
Now in your future I testify
Had you ever wondered of the days to face you
Now in your future you wish I was lying.
I'm not lying.

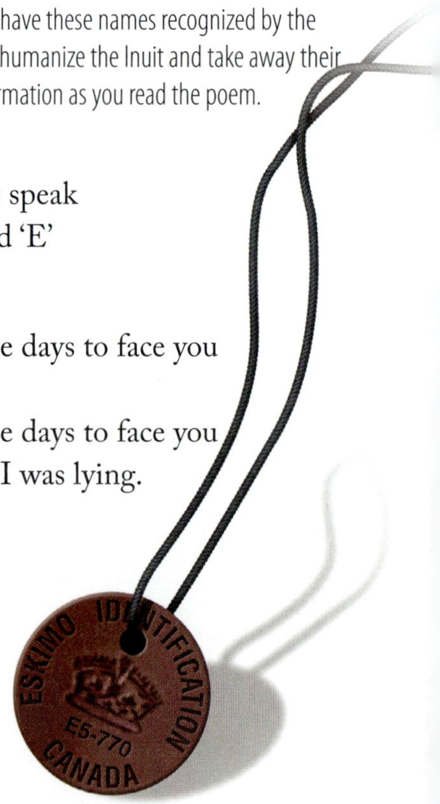

You farmed my mother, E5-770
You imposed your name number
E5-770, my mother's name.

Your tongue unfit, too frail to speak
Identities of thousands cattled 'E'
E5-770, my mother's name.

And what beautiful number
Would I be called by, born unto, tagged?

You farmed my mother, E5-770
You imposed your name number
E5-770, my mother's name.

Your tongue unfit, too frail to speak
Identities of thousands cattled 'E'
E5-770, my mother's name.

After

1. **Reading for Meaning** Who do you think is the "you" addressed in this poem? Is it always the same person/people? Why do you think this?
2. **Critical Literacy** How do you think the writer feels about her mother being named E5-770? What words and phrases from the poem make you think this?
3. **Reading for Meaning** What do you think the writer means by the line, "Your tongue unfit, too frail to speak"?
4. **Student Voice** Do you connect with the writer's feelings about something being imposed on her and her family? Why or why not?
5. **Understanding Form and Style** The words in "E5-770" are lyrics for a song. Why might you be able to guess these are song lyrics just by reading the words?
6. **Metacognition** Which of the following helped you the most in understanding the poem: acquiring background knowledge about the Inuit numbering system, analyzing words and phrases from the poem, or making inferences? Explain your choice.

Beyond

Reading for Meaning In 1969 the government of the Northwest Territories launched Project Surname, which registered Inuit under surnames instead of numbers. Research Project Surname and report on the reasons for this project and how the project was completed. Express your findings through song lyrics, a poem, a magazine article, or a dramatic presentation.

3740166701

Poetry

Written by John Adrian McDonald

John Adrian McDonald is a sixth-generation direct descendant of Chief Mistawasis of the Plains Cree. Originally from Prince Albert, Saskatchewan, he is a writer, artist, tattoo historian, musician, playwright, actor, and activist. His artwork and writing have been nominated for several awards, including the 2001 SaskTel Aboriginal Youth Achievement Award. He lives with his wife, daughter, and triplets in northern Saskatchewan.

Tips

ethno-eccentrics: a term that combines *ethnocentric* and *eccentric*. *Ethnocentric* means having a belief in the superiority of one's own ethnic group; *eccentric* means a person of odd or unconventional behaviour.

treaty card: also known as Status card; an identification card issued by the Canadian government for Status Indians

sweetgrass: one of four sacred medicines that are used to give thanks and to purify space and self with positive energy

***Tribal Trails*:** a Christian-based First Nations TV show

Before

What does it mean to you to be labelled as a student, a girl or boy, a teenager, or a member of an ethnic group? What stereotypes are associated with those labels?

During

The title of the poem, *3740166701*, is the number on the poet's treaty card. As you read the poem, think about why the poet may have chosen this as his title.

Tell me
Where is it written
In this oral tradition
That what I create
Is subject to such dictations
Lorded over by some sort
Of ethno-eccentrics
That says because you are brown
You must paint nothing but eagles
And sing nothing but powwow
And write nothing but how good
It is to be Native
And how badly we were treated
By the government and churches
And how tasty bannock is
Which isn't even Native
And even why I have to proclaim
My genetic life story

Why does this scene
Want my treaty card to precede me?
Why am I evil
If I say I don't want to?

Why can't I be me
Who just happens to be Cree?
Why can't my style stand apart
From all this souvenir-stand art?
I do not hate what I am
I just don't live by sweetgrass plans
I am not brown and acting black
I don't watch *Tribal Trails* or scream at you
To give our land back

I am what I am
First and above all
In this life of mine
Being brown is an afterthought

What Inspired Me to Write This Selection

> I wrote this poem because I feel that Aboriginal people who aren't willing to wear their heritage on their sleeve are looked down upon by those who do. I also wrote it in protest of the way that Aboriginal artists are pigeon-holed into certain genres of art and music. I feel that we as Aboriginal people are dictated to and trapped by our own stereotypes and stigmas.

After

1. **Reading for Meaning** What words and phrases does the poet associate with stereotypes of First Nations people?
2. **Critical Literacy** Whom do you think the poet is referring to when he says *ethno-eccentrics*? Support your answer with evidence from the poem.
3. **Understanding Form and Style** What effect does the poet's use of rhyme and rhythm have in the poem?
4. **Metacognition** How did knowing the title is the poet's treaty card number help you understand the poem?

Beyond

Student Voice Create a visual, oral, or written representation of your own identity. You may want to contrast your own identity with the identity you believe is expected of you.

The Amazing Sense of SHAKE

Short Story

Written by Cherie Dimaline

Illustrated by The EagleSpeaker Connection

Cherie Dimaline (Ojibway/Métis) is the writer-in-residence for First Nations House at the University of Toronto. She has spent time working for the government, running a Native Friendship Centre, writing and editing for a major Canadian women's magazine, curating a police museum, and even had a stint as a magician's assistant. Her first book, *Red Rooms,* was published in 2007. Since then, she has travelled the world and written stories that may or may not have to do with the adventures she encountered along the way. Cherie lives in Toronto, Ontario, with her three kids, two dogs, two ferrets, and one blind rat. She collects books, teacups, and tattoos.

Tips

shaking tent: a traditional sacred ceremony practised by many First Nations peoples, which involves invoking spirits to assist and answer questions

Criss Angel: an American magician

simile: a comparison made using the words *like* or *as*

Before

What insight does the title give you into the content of the story? Brainstorm your ideas.

During

As you read, write down questions you have about the story as it develops. Are there any details you would include that were left out?

With great power comes great responsibility.
—Uncle Owen, Spiderman

Before I found my own "gift," being with my Great Auntie Bernice was the closest I'd ever been to anyone exceptional. But she was less than invincible. To slow her down, all you had to do was cook her baloney extra tough. Then she had to mince it up with a butter knife because she had only gums to chew with after her false teeth were shattered in the bottom of her handbag in the accident. That was what turned her from ordinary into extraordinary—the accident, not the minced baloney. Ever since then, Auntie Bernice has been considered the traditional one in the family.

The accident happened one Wednesday in the middle of April, two years ago. She had hitched a ride to the bingo hall in the west end with her upstairs neighbour, an old French guy she called Pierre, even though his name was Tony. Pierre was driving a 1989 Cutlass Supreme with rust blooms stitched across the door panels and plastic wrap where the back window should have been. The seatbelt on the front passenger side was malfunctioning so Bernice just knotted the belt across her wide lap. Good thing too, because when they pulled off the main road and into the parking lot at the last minute, the car slid on its bald tires, skidded across the pavement, and smashed into a steel streetlight. Bernice got banged up pretty good, and when she woke up there was a handsome firefighter prying open her door. Pierre, he was nowhere to be found.

Bernice was mad because they wouldn't let her go into the bingo hall, even though she explained to the nice firefighters that, according to the laws of the universe, this would be the luckiest day of her bingo career—after suffering a low, she was sure to have a high. She pouted when they loaded her into the back of the ambulance, refused to give a statement to the police, and sulked when we came to meet her at the hospital.

"Bernice has suffered a good knock to the head," the doctor told us. "She should rest for a few days, and it would be best if someone from the family stayed with her during this time. Bring her in if things change, if she gets confused, or has any more pain."

"Jackie, I want you to stay with me," Auntie Bernice said to me.

I was surprised, and, to be honest, a little annoyed. Bernice's apartment could be on that reality show about hoarders.

"Let's go home now, dear. I want to rest." She stood up slowly, holding the side of her head where they had wrapped a spongy cotton pad with gauze to stop the bleeding from a small cut above her ear.

I was shocked by her docility, but I should have known better.

"Thank God we escaped," Bernice said, as soon as we were in the car. "Damn doctors give me the willies." She was already unwrapping the gauze around her head.

"Auntie! What are you doing? Leave that on."

"Shut up now, my girl. This is no time to talk. We can still make the 11:00 bingo session if you step on it." She applied pink lipstick in the side mirror and fluffed out her short, grey perm.

"I refuse to take you to bingo." I turned into the left-hand lane and headed toward her neighbourhood instead. "You are going home to bed."

"I'll just get out as soon as you stop, and take a cab there. And I'll be alone, so no one will know if I'm hurt. The cabbie will probably just rob me and dump my body somewhere down at the lakeshore. But if that's what you want ..."

"FINE! But we're only staying for an hour."

Halfway to the hall, Bernice started humming a pow-wow tune. "Turn up the radio there, this is a good song."

"Auntie, I don't have the radio on." I looked at her, drumming her fingers on her leg and nodding her head to some unheard music. "Maybe we should just get you home after all."

"No, no, I'm fine. Better than fine—I hear the big drum in my head, right in this ear here." She patted the side of her head with dry blood still caked into her curls. "It's a good sign. You'll see."

Auntie won $5000 that night. I got $100 for my trouble and she got a great story on top of the dough. And that drum? She still hears it. It's like her entire life has a pow-wow soundtrack. Now everyone in the family goes to Bernice for advice, thinking she has some sort of closer connection to the great mystery and all. She doesn't pretend otherwise, and even started wearing a deer-hide medicine pouch around her neck and talking with her eyes closed like she's reading real important, real Indian things off an internal teleprompter. I know for a fact she carries only bus tokens in that pouch, though.

* * *

A week before I found my own gift, I met my cousin Wauby at the coffee shop. I locked my bike outside and found her sitting by the fake fireplace in the back, doing her best to look sophisticated while drinking hot chocolate with an inordinate amount of whipped cream piled on top. I let her prattle on about school for a bit until I cut in.

"Wauby, ever feel like things are, I don't know, evolving, and we're becoming the old version? Like we're not equipped to deal with whatever's coming next?"

She had a suspicious look on her face. "What do you mean, the old version? We're not even twenty yet. There's nothing old about us."

"I mean, what would we do if the world ended right now?"

"I would finish this flippin' hot chocolate in a hurry." She licked at the whipped cream mustache on her upper lip.

"Come on, now. I'm serious! What if suddenly everything was gone, just gone? How would we be able to survive?" I stood up from my seat and grabbed her sleeve. I wasn't sure where it was coming from, but still, out it came, like these were deep thoughts I had been harbouring all along instead of sudden sentiments that were a surprise even to me.

The other patrons turned to look at us as I clutched her in near hysteria, but it didn't faze Wauby. Nothing fazed Wauby.

She looked me in the eye and said, "We're Native. We're good at surviving." Then she tilted her wide chin like she was daring anyone to say otherwise.

"Wauby," I sighed. "You threatened to move to the States when your cable was down for one lousy day."

"That was different." She looked hurt by the accusation. "*Glee* was on."

I cocked an eyebrow.

"What?" She frowned. "That's my favourite show!"

* * *

By the time I got back to the apartment, the sky was navy blue. I let myself in and turned on the TV for background noise. Mom was working the late shift again and I hated the feeling of an empty house. I flopped down on the couch, threw a blanket over my legs, and flipped through the channels, finally settling on music videos.

The dream seeped into reality like spilled milk pooling over a linoleum floor.

I was on the couch, music videos dancing and flashing, the scratchy pillow Auntie Bernice embroidered still tucked under my head. Suddenly, a plate I had left on the coffee table dropped onto the hardwood floor. As I leaned over the side of the couch to examine the damage, the framed picture from my parents' wedding day jumped off the wall and crashed to the floor, sending shards of glass skittering.

I sat up in a hurry and felt the room move, as if the couch had turned into a mechanical bull. Grey static screamed from the TV screen. From the kitchen I heard

tinkling as the cutlery drawer slid open and its contents clattered about.

Then it got bad.

Plaster and dust fell from the ceiling, the walls cracked open like an evil grin, and the pipes in the kitchen burst, sending water rushing over the counter and onto the floor. I crawled toward my bedroom, crunching over glass and strewn papers. I paused over the front section of a newspaper that had fallen off the ottoman and read the headline: *"Destruction & Death! Earthquake Hits Southern Ontario!"* An earthquake! So that's what was going on! I saw flashes of blood and body parts, eyeballs rolling away, and screaming kids.

I looked back down at the paper. Above the headline was a date: June 23, 2010. Tomorrow.

BANG!

My head hit the coffee table as I fell to the floor, and jolted me awake. For a minute, struggling under a tangled blanket, I thought I was still in the middle of the earthquake. In fact, I was halfway out the front door, whimpering and frantic, before I noticed the earth wasn't moving, that the house was still, and that I was acting like a complete lunatic. I went back into the house and to the bathroom. I washed my face, and sat on the edge of the tub trying to catch my breath and calm down. Regaining some composure, I tried tidying up to take my mind off the dream.

But there was this certainty that sat in my gut the next morning, like a heavy meal—a sad, greasy panic that threatened to jump out of my throat at the slightest provocation. I shook in the shower, trembled trying to get dressed, and ended up turning on the talk radio station to listen for news of natural disasters. I couldn't shake the dread. By noon I had convinced myself I was okay enough to be able to leave the house. I went to the one place I felt safe besides my house: the friendship centre.

The basement of the centre was as quiet as a church. There were three tables of heads, some in tight perms, others covered with faded kerchiefs, all bent over little white cards, dabbing at the numbers called from the front of the room by the cafeteria cook.

"B, 34."

"I, 19."

I tiptoed in and took a seat across from Bernice, who didn't acknowledge me until Mary Weaselhead yelled "BINGO," waving her heavy arms above her head.

"Darn Mary Weaselhead. It better be a real bingo this time. Last week she called 'BINGO' after the first four numbers." Auntie Bernice slammed her dabber down and looked at me. "Holy, what's wrong with you? You look pale as a ghost, you."

"Well, I hit my head on the coffee table, maybe that knocked the colour out of me," I said quietly.

"Coffee table? How in the heck did you manage that?"

"Falling off the couch. I had a bad dream."

"Dreams can be messages, you know." She grasped her medicine pouch, and I heard the tokens inside jingle. "We must pay attention to the signs, you know. Tell me about it; maybe I can decode it."

So I told Auntie Bernice the whole story. By the time I was done, most of the players had abandoned their games to listen—even the bingo caller stood silent. Auntie Bernice leaned back in her chair and whispered to Mary Weaselhead, "You know, when she was a baby, her grandpa brought her to a shaking tent ceremony. She could have insight into these things. Then again, it could have affected her too, you know, like mentally." She tapped at her own permed hair while Mary, who hadn't won after all, nodded.

"It was terrible," I said. "Then when I was crawling away, I passed over the newspaper and the headline said 'EARTHQUAKE' and that there had been lots of damage and injuries. And the date on the paper was June 23. That's today."

Now the whole room was quiet, hanging on every word. A few kids from the youth program had stopped in the hallway and leaned in the doorway to listen.

Then I went even further. I couldn't stop myself. I gave voice to the thing that had made me shake, the thought that, if I was going to be truthful, had brought me to the centre in the first place to warn people. "I think it's going to happen. I think we're going to have an earthquake. And I think we need to get ready."

Mary Weaselhead snorted first, then it rippled down the table to the hallway, and the boys standing in the doorway came into the room, laughing and pointing. Skyler Johnston yelled, "Check it out, we got our own seer, here. Hey medicine woman, when are the aliens going to land? Ha ha!"

I felt heat drying up the sweat on my neck. I was so humiliated. Even the old people got in on the joke.

"Oh, Jackie," sweet Mr. Blackstar said. "I had a dream last night that I smelled real bad and was left in the corner of a dark cave. Does that mean a bear is going to eat me in my sleep and then crap me out later? Maybe I should get that extra deadbolt on my apartment door, eh?"

The laughter got louder then. In fact, I saw a few tears running down wrinkled cheeks. I put my hands on the table in front of me and was about to push the chair back to leave when my Auntie beat me to it, standing up taller than she had in a long time.

"That was no dream, Blackstar, you do smell bad, and I've seen your apartment. You'd be better off in a cave." This shut down some of the guffaws, scaring people into silence, afraid they'd be the next to catch it.

"As for the rest of you, how dare you laugh at my niece? Who are you to judge anyone else?" She put a hand on my shoulder. It steadied me and I felt a little safer for it.

"Now who's to say that Jackie didn't see a real earthquake? Yes, yes," she raised her hand to stop anyone from bickering over the absurdity of it. "I understand how crazy that sounds, I'm not simple, me. But who knows, maybe there's one going on in a faraway place—maybe China or Arizona—and she sees that. But who are we to know any better?"

Silence.

"Maybe instead of being jerks we could just believe, because what's better than believing? You all lead such interesting lives that you don't have room for magic no more, eh? You all meeting big movie stars for lunch? You all travelling off on hot air balloons to meet the Wizard of Oz after bingo?"

There were a few chuckles sprinkled throughout the room, but by now the viciousness had been rubbed smooth.

"I didn't think so. Maybe we can't see things that are happening because we're too mean, trying to be all reasonable and normal. Bah! What fun is there in that?"

She waved off the notion of sanity like a gnat.

"I say the hell with being normal. I say, bring on the magic."

Mary Weaselhead clapped, "Hurray!" She quieted down when she saw she was alone. But a few people nodded their heads, and old Mr. Blackstar reached across the table to squeeze my hand.

And then it happened. The growl began in your feet, like a huge bus was driving by at top speed. A tea saucer sitting near the edge of one of the tables toppled onto the floor. Then the chairs started to jump and shimmy with the old people still in them.

When the microphone rolled onto the floor, a sharp bang and a drawn-out whistle echoed through the room. The small cage that held the white bingo balls tipped over, and they spilled off the table and bounced across the floor like eyeballs. Someone's juice box fell on its side and red liquid dripped out, pooling around the table leg. A couple of kids in the hallway held each other and screamed. Then, just as suddenly as it built up, it faded away. The screams died down, and the caller picked up the mike and switched it off.

There were a few more rumbles, like the scraping of so many chair legs, and then nothing. Just nothing.

Incredibly, the first sound was laughter. It was Auntie Bernice. She giggled, slapped her knee, and then leaned across the table, "Hey Blackstar, guess you'd better get that extra lock, eh? Ha ha!"

The story has since become Auntie Bernice's, another tale in the Indian folklore collection she busts out on special occasions, or any old time she's asked. She swears it was the bump on the head I got that knocked the gift loose, just like her. "Not that I recommend banging your noggin for fun, no, in fact, it's a rare thing to begin with. You can't fall on your head and hope to be Criss Angel, there. No, you have to be born with it, like me and Jackie."

It was a small earthquake that hit north of Ottawa. What we felt were just minor tremors—aftershocks, really. And I don't feel different, really. There are no drums or epiphanies, and I certainly haven't turned into some kind of magician. In fact, my particular specialty renders me kind of useless. There's not much need for an earthquake spotter in this part of the world.

The best part is the knowing. Just knowing that at any moment there could be a little piece of the extraordinary caught up in the most ordinary of days.

After

1. **Reading for Meaning** Identify the most important ideas being presented in this story.
2. **Critical Literacy** What does the author want the reader to think of Auntie Bernice? Explain, using examples from the story.
3. **Reading for Meaning** What do you think the author is trying to say about traditional beliefs in a contemporary context?
4. **Understanding Form and Style** In what ways do you think humour contributes to this short story? How do you think it helps to convey the message of the story?
5. **Understanding Form and Style** Identify two or three similes that the author uses in this story. Do you think these similes are effective? Explain why or why not.
6. **Metacognition** What strategies did you use to help you better understand the story?

Beyond

Student Voice The narrator in this story says, "The best part is the knowing. Just knowing that at any moment there could be a little piece of the extraordinary caught up in the most ordinary of days." Can you describe a day where you experienced the extraordinary? Share this experience, or one that you make up, in a creative format.

From Chef Kai's Kitchen

Autobiography and Recipe

Written by Kai Zyganiuk

Kai Zyganiuk has been a chef for fourteen years, working in some of the finest restaurants around the world. He was born to a West Indian father and a Native Canadian/Polish mother in Toronto, Ontario, and has been a long-time resident of Wasauksing First Nation, Parry Island, Ontario.

Tip

ANDPVA: abbreviation for Association for Native Development in the Performing and Visual Arts, an organization that provides support to Canadian First Nations, Inuit, and Métis artists in Ontario and around the world

Before

What types of skills and knowledge must a successful chef possess? Do you believe that this selection about Chef Kai will affirm or challenge your predictions?

During

As you read the selection, think about the format of a recipe. How is it different from other genres of writing?

My Culinary Journey

Since the age of sixteen, I have been working my way up the ranks in the exciting and ever-changing culinary world. Born in Toronto, Ontario, to a West Indian father and Native Canadian/Polish mother, I was inspired to pursue cooking by my grandmother on my mother's side, an incredible home cook who prepared everything with love. Throughout my career, I have worked for some of Toronto's top fine-dining establishments and private clubs including the Granite Club, the Oakdale Golf and Country Club, Pure Spirits, the Four Seasons Hotel (Truffles), the Spoke Club (which I opened with chef Robert Kirk), and Cucina (where I worked as head chef).

My intense focus, constant thirst for knowledge, and extreme love for everything food, have contributed to my fourteen-year tenure in the competitive culinary industry. During my travels, I have also performed stages at various establishments around the world such as the five-star RIU Hotel in Ocho Rios, Jamaica, and the Coogee Bay Hotel in Sydney, Australia.

Most recently, my culinary passion brought me to Los Angeles, California, where I worked in a number of fast-paced kitchens. During my one-year stay, I worked as the executive chef for one of Hollywood's premier private clubs.

My cooking style is local, seasonal, and diversified with a French influence. The most important aspects of any meal are the quality of the products, correct seasoning and cooking techniques, and presentation. A great chef is also aware that less is more. Cooking is something that one must truly love in order to produce great-tasting meals. One of the joys of being a chef is watching the reaction of satisfied guests. That validates what I do every day.

With a cookbook currently in the works, radio interviews under my belt, and a interest in both video and television production, I was selected as one of sixteen top Canadian chefs for Canada's first chef reality TV series, *The Pressure Cooker*.

I work with First Nations youth as the food and nutrition instructor at Native Child and Family Services of Toronto. I am a proud Aboriginal band member and long-time resident of Wasauksing First Nation, Parry Island. As a member of ANDPVA, I am recognized for my dedication to working with and making a difference in the community.

Lamb Burgers with Summer Salad

Ingredients

Lamb Burgers

- 2 lb (1 kg) medium ground lamb
- 1 ripe avocado
- 2 roma tomatoes
- 1 bunch watercress, or pea shoots
- Half wheel of Brie, Brie du meaux or Camembert cheese
- 1 tsp (5 mL) cumin seeds
- 1/2 cup (125 mL) ketchup
- Salt and pepper to taste
- Some really fresh buns

Salad

- 2 carrots
- 1 grapefruit
- Baby radishes
- Baby arugula

Vinaigrette

- 1 tbsp (15 mL) real maple syrup
- 1/2 cup (125 mL) light olive oil
- Juice and zest of 1 lemon
- Salt and pepper to taste

Instructions

Lamb Burgers

1. Place the meat in a bowl. Mix in 1/2 tsp of salt and pepper each. Mix well.
2. Form a tiny portion of meat (1/2 oz or 15 g) into a patty. Cook the patty fully and taste to check the seasoning. Add more salt and pepper if needed.
3. Form the burgers. Each burger can be 4 oz to 8 oz (125 g to 250 g). Let the burgers sit in the fridge for a minimum of 30 minutes to set firm.
4. The burgers can be grilled or baked, but grilling them allows for much more caramelization and a smoky flavour. Test the patty with a meat thermometer. To be fully cooked, it should read 160°F, or 150°F if you want it a bit juicer.
5. While the burgers are cooking, slice the avocado, tomatoes, and Brie, and wash and dry the watercress.
6. Toast the cumin seeds in a nonstick pan on low heat. Then grind the cumin in a spice grinder.
7. Add cumin to ketchup. Add salt and pepper to taste.
8. When burgers are cooked, top them with avocado, tomatoes, watercress, Brie, and cumin seed ketchup.

Salad and Vinaigrette

1. Use a different cutting board than the one used for the meat to avoid cross-contamination. Peel the carrots and slice them into fine strips (julienne).
2. Peel the grapefruit. Using a small paring knife, cut between the membranes on each side of the grapefruit segments. The individual segments will release. Discard the membranes.
3. Thinly slice the baby radishes. Be careful! You can use a grater instead.
4. To prepare the salad dressing, whisk the maple syrup into the olive oil in a steady stream. Add the lemon juice and zest, and salt and pepper and whisk until fully incorporated. Taste for seasoning and enjoy!

What Inspired Me to Create This Recipe

> "I created the Lamb Burger with Summer Salad recipe for everyone to enjoy. It's simple, delicious, and demands the attention of any burger lover. As a chef, my quest for the best, most flavourful burger has been exciting and ongoing. Throughout my travels in Australia and North America, I have tried an incredible variety of burgers. However, I would have to say that some of the most memorable burgers I ever tried were in Los Angeles. And no, it wasn't because of the trendy boutiques that lined the streets or the notable chefs whose names graced the storefront signage. It came, however, from the passion that I had for the best possible burger by simply using the freshest of ingredients and treating them with respect—period!
>
> To begin, it's best to start with your local butcher where you can purchase local ground lamb. In my case, it's Ontario lamb. Next, be sure to use fresh, seasonal garnishes and a good bun."

After

1. **Critical Literacy** Describe how Chef Kai reveals aspects of his personality through his biography, recipe, and inspiration. Pay particular attention to what he includes and doesn't include in his biography.
2. **Student Voice** Which parts of Chef Kai's life made the greatest impression on you? Why?
3. **Reading for Meaning** Are the steps in the recipe clear? Do you think any information is missing? If so, what changes would you recommend?
4. **Metacognition** How does reading a recipe help you read other step-by-step texts (such as experiments, instruction manuals, directions)?

Beyond

1. **Creating Media Texts** Create a profile for a new cooking show. Include a cooking theme for the first show and a look for the show's set. Create an advertisement for the show that would appear in a magazine or on television.
2. **Student Voice** Brainstorm what a fulfilling life would look like for you. Then write a recipe for living a fulfilling life.

spiders

Poetry

Written by Sharron Proulx-Turner

Sharron Proulx-Turner is a member of the Métis Nation of Alberta. Originally from the Ottawa river valley, Ontario, Sharron is from Mohawk, Wyandat, Algonquin, Ojibway, Mi'kmaw, French, and Irish ancestry. She's a two-spirit *nokomis* (grandmother), mom, writer, and community worker. Her work appears in several anthologies and her books have been finalists for numerous awards.

Tips

infinity symbol: symbolizes the joining of two cultures and the existence of a people forever. The infinity symbol appears on the Métis flag.

medicine wheel: a circle divided into four sections, each representing a direction. It is a symbol of harmony and peaceful interaction among all living beings on earth, and is also known as the holistic wheel.

two-spirit person: a person born one sex who fulfills the roles assigned to both sexes, or other roles reserved for two-spirit people. Some people consider two-spirit a term that can refer to lesbian, gay, bisexual, and transgender people. The definition of a two-spirit person varies across First Nations, Inuit, and Métis cultures.

Before

Think back to a dream that had a positive impact on you. Write a short description of the dream and why it had an impact.

During

As you read, visualize what the poet is describing. What words and phrases helped you create the pictures in your mind?

> *The spider's web is a physical construct which many native cultures draw on symbolically to imbed this principle in their storytelling as an expression of the creative process concerned with the connectedness of all things.*
>
> —Jeannette Armstrong, Syilx poet and educator, and Douglas Cardinal, Métis architect

first thing this morning
a brown striped spider
crossed my path
between my bedroom and the bath

I picked her up, thanked her,
her, afraid of my dry, salt-palm
I put her outside
her body the shape of Métis
infinity, family,
her eight legs
the four directions of the wind
the medicine wheel

not ten minutes earlier
between waking and asleep
I dreamed I was inside my house
inside my heart and body
where spirit resides
where each season
each rock and tree and leaf
listens to the sound that life makes
within these walls

I dreamed my house fell
face first
onto the ground
baby spiders all around

I was reminded of last summer
a large black spider, weighted down
by her babies on her back
so many tiny eyes looking up
into mine

they seemed to be talking
all talking at once, their voices
a quiet drone, a storyteller's tone
the storyteller's role is to draw a story
out of the listener, they said
all in unison, not an illusion

Grandmother Spider Connects All Life Together
by Aaron Paquette

I kept blinking my eyes against the sun
sweat pooling inside my ears
and I heard them again
they said, a great deal of a story
is there, you see, inside the listener

two young two-spirit girls walked up just then
their eyes wide, their joy like a tune
their laughter, loud and long
filling the spaces, pushing their voices down
through their bellies and feet through the ground

they'd written a play, those two young two-spirit girls
a play about the winds of change
performed that play for the spiders there
their little black bodies moving in time
to the movements of the two-spirit girls

who joined together their bodies
in an eight-legged dance
weaving the future
a spider's web, heart-shaped
life's strength, all nations
all races, all genders
all ours, they said

the two young two-spirit girls
their downward voices beating, beating
we got the rhythm of the planet, us
we got the road to peace
hey-ya-hey-ya-hey-eh-hey-ya-hey-ya-hey
hey-ya-hey-ya-hey-eh-hey-ya-hey-ya-hey
hey-ya-hey-ya-hey
hey-ya-hey-ya-hey-ya-hey-hey-hey-yo

What Inspired Me to Write This Selection

"Elders tell us that there was a time when people who carried two spirits—female and male—were esteemed and respected in most Indigenous societies. These people were often the healers, the caregivers of children, the visionaries, the medicine people. The honoured place of two-spirit people has changed drastically over the past 500 years. The poem "spiders" is like a spider web that weaves dreams, stories, and experiences from my own recent past and present, and looks into a hopeful future where the role of the two-spirits is restored once again. It is a poem that recognizes the connectedness of all peoples."

After

1. **Reading for Meaning** How do the two young two-spirit girls view the world and the future? Support your answer with evidence from the poem.
2. **Reading for Meaning**
   a) What connections between the spiders and the two-spirit girls does the poet make?
   b) Why do you think she makes those connections?
3. **Understanding Form and Style** How impactful was the poet's use of metaphor in this poem? How do these metaphors contribute to the meaning of the poem?
4. **Reading for Meaning** In the poem, the spiders say, "the storyteller's role is to draw a story / out of the listener ... a great deal of a story / is there, you see, inside the listener." How does this statement relate to the theme of connectedness of all things?
5. **Critical Literacy** In what ways does this poem and the poet's statement of inspiration give voice to views that are often silent?
6. **Metacognition** What parts of the poem were clear to you? What parts did you find confusing? What did you do to clarify your confusion?

Beyond

Student Voice What image from the poem had the greatest impact on you? Why do you think that is the case? Create a diorama of that particular scene. Include a line or stanza from the poem that describes the scene.

Waawaate Fobister: A Shining Star

Biography

Written by Lisa Charleyboy

Lisa Charleyboy is Tsilhqot'in, of Raven Clan, from Alexis Creek First Nation, British Columbia. Currently living in Toronto, Ontario, she has recently graduated from York University with a Bachelor of Arts Honours Degree in Professional Writing. Lisa also is a freelance writer and moonlights as the Urban Native Girl, who has her own Indigenous pop culture blog.

Tip

pow-wow grass dance: a form of men's dancing at a pow-wow involving colourful regalia that resembles a field in motion. The grass dance documents the journey of a man preparing land to camp in a respectful way.

Before

This selection is a short biography. What type of information do you expect to read about in this selection?

During

As you read, think about the obstacles Waawaate had to overcome in order to be successful. How do you think he was able to move forward?

When it comes to choosing which college or university to attend, many high school students spend months carefully looking over pamphlets and Web sites, figuring out which school and program will be the perfect fit.

Waawaate Fobister had a different journey. His guidance counsellor came into his Grade Twelve classroom on the deadline day for college applications, leaving him with only two hours to make this life-changing decision. Lucky for him, he knew that drama was his calling, and applied to every theatre program in Ontario.

That was the entry onto a path that led Waawaate to win six Dora Mavor Moore Awards. It's the highest honour in Canadian theatre, and Waawaate earned them when he was only 25 years old. The acclaim was for his 2009 debut play, *Agokwe*. It was an amazing feat, since the play started as a ramble during an open-mic night.

He developed it into a monologue, and eventually into the 70-minute play it is today. Waawaate never imagined that his ramble would turn into such a huge success.

Agokwe is a one-man show, in which Waawaate plays all seven characters. The play is about a two-spirited, pow-wow grass dancer who has a crush on another boy, a hockey player. But ultimately this "gay love on the rez" story doesn't end well, and the main character faces social isolation and homophobia.

The story's content stemmed from conflict within Waawaate's own life. He says that his two main characters "could not feel and be who they are in today's Native and mainstream society because the teachings and lifestyle of Native people is gone."

Historically, in Native tradition, two-spirited people were considered gifted, because they carried the spirits of both male and female. They were often medicine people, visionaries, and healers in precolonial societies. To understand Waawaate's perspective on this modern shift away from inclusion in Native society, it's important to explore some of his own history.

Waawaate grew up on his home reservation, Grassy Narrows, (located one hour north of Kenora, Ontario) until he left for college in Toronto at age eighteen. His reserve had only 1000 people, so his community was tight-knit and everybody knew everybody else. This can be a very good thing, but when you're the focus of gossip, like Waawaate was, it can be devastating.

"I was teased and bullied. Even adults would like to pick on me," he says. "I was once at my grandparents' house and there was this older lady sitting on the balcony who kept saying, 'You look like a girl.' She probably said that like fifteen times, and kept asking me why. The people at the party were laughing. I remember feeling bullied by that lady. I was only ten or eleven years old."

Waawaate says he was quite feminine while growing up and thought he had a girlish face. He played with Barbies and was more interested in hopscotch with the girls than whatever the other boys were doing.

When he was fifteen, Waawaate was badly beaten by another teenage boy on the reserve who didn't approve of him being two-spirited. Waawaate's injuries were so serious that he was in the hospital for nearly a week.

But that didn't hold him back. He was the first person in his family to graduate from high school; he was one of only five students from his community in his graduating class. That perseverance helped when he decided to move away from home and study theatre.

Waawaate's transition from a small First Nations community to the Big Smoke (as Toronto is sometimes called) was a hard one. Waawaate explains that "my social skills were really lacking. I was really awkward. I had no non-Native friends before coming here. I was the only Native student in that [theatre] program." So Waawaate reached out to the Native community by going to the Native Canadian Centre and started making friends there.

He says that living in Toronto at first was scary, but exciting. "I had to deal with a lot of homesickness. It almost took me down." He came close to dropping out of school to return home because he felt awkward, isolated, and insecure about himself and his sexuality.

But the struggles in his first year helped him to find the courage to come out, and he officially told his family about his sexual identity. His dad was supportive and saw how much weight was lifted off Waawaate's shoulders by telling people. "He just told me that he loved me no matter what, and that I should continue whatever I am doing in my life," Waawaate says. "He said to shoot for the stars."

Waawaate Fobister

And that's exactly what Waawaate did. Once he finished college, he took the advice he received from other Native actors who told him, "The best way to get the work that you want to do is to write your own stuff."

"That's what I wanted to do in the beginning anyway. I wanted to share because I am a storyteller," he says. It's this strong and proud oral tradition of Native people that runs through Waawaate, and he's been able to develop his gift by translating those stories into award-winning performances. Since he actively chose to pursue theatre as his major, and make his way to the Big Smoke, he hasn't looked back. And he now looks forward with optimism.

"When I go back home, I look for the storyteller in each person, so they can find their voice again," he says. "A lot of our Native people are lost. They're stuck between places and they've lost their voices." Waawaate is doing his part to help restore those voices through the magic of theatre.

After

1. **Reading for Meaning** Why does Waawaate believe that First Nations two-spirited people face challenges today that they did not face in the past?
2. **Critical Literacy**
   a) What does the author say to try to get the reader to like and relate to Waawaate? Provide specific examples from the selection.
   b) How do you think the author views Waawaate? Explain your thinking.
3. **Student Voice** Have you witnessed or experienced bullying or feelings of isolation in your own life? If so, how have you dealt with these situations?
4. **Understanding Form and Style** Describe the author's writing style. What have you learned from her writing that you may apply to your own?
5. **Metacognition**
   a) How did knowing this selection was a biography help you to understand it better?
   b) Did this selection fulfil your expectations of a biography?

Beyond

Listening and Speaking Interview a friend or family member. Create a biography about that person using a method of your choice, such as a magazine article, song, poster, or play.

West

Taking a Stand

BIG IDEA

What would you stand up for?

The West represents elements of fall, introspection, the intellectual aspects of a person, and the adult phase of personal development.

In this section, First Nations and Métis peoples share their personal connection to and experience with social justice issues, historical, and current events, and relationships to the self, others, the environment and government. You'll meet Rabbit as she demonstrates what it takes to be a leader; you'll see how age-old stories become cutting-edge fashion in the hands of a skilled designer, and you'll get a recipe for reconciling the past with the present.

Stories in this section show the strengths of First Nations and Métis peoples as we continuously stand up for our rights. The authors give alternative perspectives on current affairs and their historical underpinnings. Through these stories of courage and commitment, you'll discover how struggles can become strengths and how your strengths help you overcome your struggles. Then you'll be challenged to consider your own role in those struggles and contemplate where you stand.

My Whole Life Going Home

Poetry

Written by Al Hunter

Al Hunter is a citizen of the Anishnaabe Nation within Treaty 3 and a proud member of the Caribou clan. He has served his community in many ways, including as chief, land claim negotiator, environmental issues advisor, writer, high school counsellor, college and university instructor, and healing and wellness co-ordinator. His poetry has been widely published in anthologies and journals. He lives in Rainy River First Nations, Ontario.

Before

What does the word *home* mean to you?

During

While reading the poem, think about questions that you would like to ask the poet. Predict how he might respond to your questions.

Tip

Aleut: native to the Aleutian Islands and coastal areas of southwestern Alaska

One beautiful evening in June,
I met an Aleut woman in the small dining room
of an old elegant hotel.
We were two Indians in Washington, DC,
each having dinner alone.
We nodded to one another across the room the way
Indians do, a silent acknowledgement and an invitation.
After introductions, we shared a table.
While the waiter brought us water,
appetizers, and entrees all served elegantly,
she told me of the windswept arctic islands,
the islands she and the Aleut people called home.
"I've spent my whole life going home," she said.

What Inspired Me to Write This Selection

"I was inspired by the woman's story and her commitment to her community and people, the *Aleuts* (*Unangan*). From her community off the coast of Alaska to Washington, DC, where I met her, is a 6500-km trip, and takes days of travel. She travelled regularly to the United States capital on behalf of her people."

After

1. **Reading for Meaning** Read the poem again. As you read, use the words from the poem to create a picture in your mind. What words were most helpful in creating this picture?
2. **Critical Literacy** Why do you think the poet has chosen to write about the theme of home?
3. **Reading for Meaning** What do you think the woman means when she says, "I've spent my whole life going home"?
4. **Reading for Meaning** How does the statement "We nodded to one another across the room the way Indians do, a silent acknowledgement and an invitation" help you to understand the poem?
5. **Metacognition** How did making inferences and analyzing text help you understand this selection?

Beyond

1. **Student Voice** Write about what *home* means to you. It may be in the form of a poem, a paragraph, or lyrics in a song.
2. **Student Voice** Create a visual representation (such as a video, slide show, or other multimedia presentation) of your home town or community. How does your community compare to the Aleut woman's community?

Young Couple by Jim Logan

The Animal People Choose a Leader

Short Story

Written by Richard Wagamese

Illustrated by Kristy Cameron

Richard Wagamese is Ojibway from the Wabaseemoong First Nation in northwestern Ontario. Self-educated and self-taught, he is the author of nine titles in memoir and novel form, in addition to a new book of poetry. Richard has won journalism and publishing awards and is an acclaimed public speaker. He lives outside Kamloops, British Columbia, with his wife and dog.

Tips

anthropomorphism: giving human characteristics to something that is not human, such as an animal or inanimate object. The author's use of anthropomorphism in this story is characteristic of traditional First Nations, Inuit, and Métis storytelling.

third-person narrator: a person who is not a character in the story and who tells the story from that perspective

Before

Reflect on the title of the story. Make predictions about the content and potential characters.

During

While reading the story, create a timeline of the race. Think about how this strategy assists you in understanding the selection.

In the Long Ago Time when there was just the Animal People, they decided that they needed to choose a leader. They held a meeting in a great meadow and there was much sage discussion about how this would happen. All members of the animal kingdom were there: birds, reptiles, insects, and all of the four-leggeds. This was in the time when the Animal People could speak to each other with one mind in one common language so even the fish and those that swim could be heard. It was a very solemn occasion.

"A leader must be strong and proud," said Buffalo and the entire circle murmured at his wisdom.

"A leader must carry the medicine power of wisdom," said Wolverine and there was much discussion about his offering.

"Leaders must have a powerful presence. One that commands respect," said Wolf and all nodded in agreement.

Around and around the discussion went. There were many admirable suggestions about the attributes of leadership but no one could come up with a process for choosing. The Animal People lived in harmony and the idea of creating a hierarchy, of elevating one over the other, was beyond them. As the talk continued, they became discouraged and wondered if there was a respectful and honourable way to choose a leader. The day lengthened and evening started to slide across the sky, and still there was no consensus.

Then a small voice spoke. Everyone strained to hear, and when the voice was located, the Animal People separated and made way for the speaker to come forward. A small squirrel, Ajidimo, hopped slowly to the front of the throng and stood in the middle of the great circle of her peers. "There should be a race," Ajidimo said. "A race would show who exemplifies the qualities of leadership. A race requires perseverance, fortitude, strength, and a powerful will."

The circle of animals launched into a babble of discussion. Everyone was excited by this new possibility and, of course, many of the animals came forward to enter the race.

"It will be me," said Horse. "With my fleetness and strength, I will overcome any challenge and I will emerge the leader."

"You think too highly of yourself, my brother," said Buffalo. "It will be I who emerges victorious for no one has more stamina."

"What's needed is a discerning manner," said Cougar. "Your power is no match for my ability to cover territory with stealth. I will emerge as the leader because of my gift of patience."

"None can match my stealth," said Wolverine. "No one knows how to move secretly as much as I."

When no one else came forward, Eagle (who declined to enter the race because of his role as Messenger, carrying all prayers to Creator) called for quiet. He flapped down from the topmost branches of the tree he sat in and conferred with Mukwa the bear and Myeengun the wolf. They talked a long while. Finally, Eagle hopped into the centre of the circle and addressed the throng.

"There is a lake set between a circle of steep hills," Eagle said. "I have flown over it many times and it forms a perfect circle. The terrain is challenging: rocky, steep with thick woods around it. The race will be four times around that lake. This will demand the utmost of the contestants, and the winner will indeed be the hardiest and most qualified to lead us."

The Animal People concurred that this was a remarkable plan. There was much excited talk about who of the four would emerge victorious. Then Eagle spoke again.

"Are there any other challengers? Is there anyone else who would like to contest for the right to lead us?"

"I would," said Wapoose, the rabbit. She hopped out of the crowd and sat looking at Eagle.

"You are small, my sister. Are you certain?" Eagle asked.

"Yes," Wapoose said. "It would be an honour to contest with such magnificent beings."

The animals worried that Wapoose was asking too much of herself, but she was determined so the five contestants headed for the lake with Eagle flying overhead as their guide. When they reached the lake, Eagle lined them up on the rocky shore. "Be careful," Eagle said. "I have never seen any of us try to navigate this lake before. The terrain is so difficult."

The bigger animals stamped hooves and clawed at the shore impatiently. Wapoose merely wriggled her nose and watched them. At a signal from Eagle, the race was on.

Horse neighed and reared up on his hind legs and then galloped off into the trees. Buffalo was right at his tail, and the others could hear them crashing through the trees. Wolverine scurried forward with his nose close to the ground and vanished like a shadow into the trees. Cougar loped easily after him and disappeared as well into the thick cover of the bush. Wapoose sat on her haunches and watched them leave, and, when she was ready, hopped off slowly into the trees. Eagle flapped up onto a ridge of rock to count the laps as they passed.

Horse and Buffalo were immensely strong and they made it back to the rocky shore in a virtual tie. They were scratched and cut from thrashing their way through the dense cover. They stopped to drink, and Cougar and Wolverine bounded out of the trees. They all drank and caught their breath and stared at each other to determine who might be wearied or weakened, or want to drop out. None of them did and they raced off on the second lap. Eagle stared back in the direction they'd come and worried about the tiny rabbit who still could not be seen. The larger animals had returned from their second lap and then raced off again before Wapoose hopped slowly from the trees.

"Oh, the land is so lovely," Wapoose said. "There is so much to see and the feeling of being on it is beautiful."

"You are far behind," Eagle said. "There is no way for you to ever catch up."

"Don't worry about me. I'm here to enjoy the challenge," Wapoose said. Then she took a small drink and continued on her way.

Eagle waited a long time for that third lap to conclude. It was Buffalo who emerged first but even his proud steps were plodding. The great animal slumped to the shore and drank thirstily, his breath between slurps coming hard and heaving. When he finished, Horse walked out of the trees. He too was worn out. They stood side by side at the water's edge while Wolverine and Cougar emerged from the dense cover together. They took sidelong glances at each other but both were far too wearied to comment or challenge the other. Instead, they stood beside the other two animals and drank slowly. When they were finished, none of the great creatures seemed too eager to continue the race. They stared at the trees blankly. It was finally Horse who stepped out first. The others watched him go and only when he'd vanished into the bush did they move to follow. Eagle could only peer back wondering how Wapoose was doing on her second lap.

The others had been gone almost an hour before Wapoose hopped out of the trees. She was bright-eyed and energetic, and none of her fur had marks of struggle like the others. Again, she took a few small sips of water and sat on the shore admiring the look of the sun on the lake's surface.

"There is no way for you to win, my sister," Eagle said. "The others are on their final lap already. Perhaps it's best if you concede and stay here and wait to greet the winner along with me."

Wapoose nodded solemnly and continued to stare out at the lake. "It is not honouring the challenge if I should stop," she said. "It is a noble pursuit and it asks everything I have. So I will continue if that's all right with you."

"Certainly," Eagle said. "I only meant to spare you unnecessary struggle."

"It can never be struggle to engage in a noble cause," Wapoose said.

She hopped off after the other creatures. Eagle flapped his great wings and settled more firmly on the branch. He admired Wapoose. The rabbit was brave and respectful and carried a very humble way of looking at the world. She would have made a remarkable leader.

As Eagle sat in the tree, Wapoose ran nimbly along under the snags and tangles that hampered the bigger creatures. When she came to huge boulders, she sat and sniffed at the wind and found the air currents that told her the easiest path to follow. Where the way seemed impassable for someone of her size, she merely sat up on her haunches and eyed the territory until she found a pathway. She'd established a route on her first two passes that allowed her to pick up speed. She blazed through open stretches and hopped boldly along the edge of chasms that seemed impossible for a creature so small. But she also took time to stop and admire the geography she passed through. She sat and gazed around at the magnificent sweep of the country and inhaled the crystalline air deeply into her, and she admired the interplay of shadow and light that was thrown everywhere around her. Then she would wriggle her nose and continue on her journey.

She hadn't gone far on her third lap when she encountered Wolverine. He was snagged in a crevice of rock where he'd been trying to take a shortcut over a ridge. He was furious, and Wapoose could hear him snarling and raging and tearing away at the rock with his long claws. But he was also very tired and he had to stop and catch his breath. During a lull, the rabbit spoke to him.

"Let go," Wapoose said. "All you have to do is let go and stop struggling. When you do, you will slide back down and you can begin again."

"What do you know, little one?" Wolverine snarled. "I am strong enough to claw my way out of here."

With that, Wolverine attacked the face of the crevice again. There was an awesome sound of claws on granite and his hard spit and snarl. But it was to no avail. He was trapped.

"Let go," Wapoose said again. "It may require all your strength to do that but it is your struggle itself that traps you."

Wolverine huffed. His breath was ragged. He peered down at Wapoose, who seemed so small at the foot of the drop. It was a long way down. He gazed up at the thin poke of blue sky at the head of the crevice, and he could feel the burning desire in him to breach it and continue the race. But he was exhausted. He took another look at Wapoose, and she seemed so calm and assured that he relaxed and quit fighting. Sure enough, Wolverine slid slowly back down the crevice and landed in the gravel and stone beside Wapoose. He flopped down on his belly and stretched his paws out. "Thank you," was all he had breath for.

Wapoose sat and waited while he regained his strength. Eventually Wolverine sat up. "It is lost," he said. "I am too tired to continue. I will not be the leader. I do not have what is required."

"The way I have found is easier," Wapoose said. "It takes longer but I make it all the way around without a struggle. I would be very happy if you accompanied me."

With that, Wolverine and Wapoose began to make their way. They hadn't travelled very far when they heard a great stamping and snorting in the trees. They followed the sound and came upon Horse tangled in a thicket of blackberry bushes. The thorns were cutting into his flesh, and the pain drove him to kick and buck relentlessly. He

was covered in sweat. Again, when Horse had ceased his immense struggle and calmed some, Wapoose spoke.

"The branches are individual," she said to Horse. "If you pass through them one at a time, there is less resistance. Taken together, they are a strong barrier."

"What do you know?" Horse asked. "You are not even in contention in this race."

"That is true but I know that barriers such as this are built of many parts," Wapoose said. "When I hop through them, I learned to be patient and push against one piece at a time. We will show you."

Wapoose led Wolverine to the edge of the thicket. She paused and directed Wolverine to place his paw against one slim branch. A line of blackberry shoots fell forward. Then she hopped a few steps further and showed Wolverine where to place another paw. More of a pathway opened up. Eventually they worked their way right up to Horse who neighed in relief and followed them back out the opening. When they stood in the clear again, Wapoose and Wolverine could see how many cuts Horse had inflicted on himself in the thicket.

"Buffalo and Cougar went by me and did not stop to help," Horse said. "That angered me. I fought against the bushes, but they would not relent."

"Things bend any number of ways," Wapoose said. "You learn this when you spend time close to the Earth as I do."

"Thank you," Horse said.

"We are travelling together now," Wapoose said. "The way I found is easier to navigate but takes more time. You're welcome to join us, of course."

"I'd like that," Horse said. "I'm very tired."

The three of them ventured off, with Wapoose hopping casually in the lead. She led them on a path that wound its way gently around and through many barriers. They were grateful for the respite. But they hadn't gone far when they could hear Buffalo snorting angrily. They followed the sound and came upon him belly deep in a bog. Buffalo kicked and thrashed, but his efforts only sank him deeper into the slick, oily muck. When he saw them on the edge of the bog, he stopped and looked at them.

"How did you come to be in there?" Horse asked.

"I thought it was a shortcut," Buffalo said. "Cougar was bounding ahead of me and I thought that I could save time by cutting through a gap. I was belly deep before I knew it."

"Can you stand?" Wapoose asked.

"Yes," Buffalo said. "Why?"

"If you can stand there calmly, you won't sink any further and we will work together to get you out of there."

"Are you certain?" Buffalo asked. "I feel the bog pull at me even now."

"I am not certain," Wapoose said. "But trust does not require certainty."

With that, she hopped to a clutch of cedar trees and worked her way among them. Horse and Wolverine followed her and watched while she searched about. She came to a tree that had a root showing through the soil. Wapoose chewed at the root, and when she'd eaten through it, she asked Wolverine to come at it with his great claws. He pawed at the soil and exposed a good length of root. Then Wapoose directed Horse to take the exposed root in his teeth and back up slowly to pull it from the ground. When he did this, they could see that there was enough root to reach out to where Buffalo stood mired in the muck.

"Take this in your teeth and swim out to Buffalo," Wapoose said to Wolverine. "Have him take it in his teeth and climb up on his back. Horse will pull you both out."

"But I might sink before I reach him," Wolverine said.

"Perhaps," said Wapoose. "But everything asks sacrifice of us. You must sacrifice your doubt now to help your brother."

"Are you sure?" Wolverine asked.

"No," Wapoose said. "But I am not the one who has to be."

Wolverine took the root in his jaws and waded into the mud. He felt it clutch at him but he worked his way slowly to Buffalo, and, while the great beast took the root in his mouth, Wolverine climbed onto his back. Slowly, Horse backed away from the edge of the bog. Horse and Wapoose could see the two of them come closer and closer to safety. Finally Buffalo's hooves caught. He struggled but walked out of the bog and stood glistening with muck. Wolverine hopped from his back and did a celebratory dance around his bigger brother.

"How did you know to find the root?" Buffalo asked.

"You discover much when you learn to look at things," Wapoose said.

Buffalo nodded. "I suppose Cougar has finished the last lap. He will be our leader now. I'm exhausted. I don't know if I can make it back."

"We have been making our way around together on the route that Wapoose found,"

Wolverine said. "It is longer, but less arduous than the ones we found. You're welcome to join us as well."

Buffalo agreed and the four friends resumed their loop around the lake. They came upon Cougar flopped on a large flat boulder, clearly exhausted. He lay on his side with his tongue lolling out and his breath coming in slow, shallow pants. His fur was matted and torn from negotiating his way through the territory, and his eyes were half closed.

"I'm spent," Cougar said when they approached him. "I went too fast for too long and the effort has robbed me of all my strength. I don't know if I have energy to stand, let alone make it to the finish line. I've failed."

"There is no failure when judgment does not exist," Wapoose said softly.

"What do you mean?" Cougar asked.

"I mean that we do not judge you. We contested with you and we have no judgment. Neither does Creator. So it is not possible for you to have failed."

"But I did not complete the journey."

"Yet." Wapoose said. "We will carry you."

Buffalo stepped up to the rock and Cougar eased onto his broad back. The five of them continued their walk around the lake. Wapoose led them along and they marvelled at the leisure they found in the route she had discovered. When Buffalo's energy flagged, he moved beside another high boulder and Horse allowed Cougar to climb onto his back. Eventually, even Wolverine was near collapse and Buffalo carried him while he rested his head on his brother's great hump. Wapoose hopped nimbly along ahead of them. Together the five contestants made their way slowly back to the shore where Eagle waited. When he saw them, he flapped his great wings in celebration. They crossed the finish line together.

"It is a great day," Eagle said when told of Wapoose's direction.

"But we do not have a leader," Wolverine said.

"I think we do," Eagle said and they all looked at Wapoose.

"Oh, I do not want to be the leader," Wapoose said.

"But you entered the contest," Buffalo said.

"I entered to learn what I did not know," said Wapoose. "I did not enter to contend."

"What was it you sought to learn?" Horse asked.

"I understood the meaning of leader," Wapoose said. "But I did not understand the territory."

"And now?" Eagle asked.

Wapoose wriggled her nose. "I understand that when all our energies are directed toward the same goal, there is no need for one to lead. We all help each other complete the journey."

"You are wise," said Eagle.

"I am Wapoose," she said. "This is all I know for certain."

"Then truly you are wise," Eagle said, and the others murmured their agreement.

Wapoose hopped off a few steps toward the line of forest at the end of the beach.

"Where are you going?" they all yelled together.

"To complete the journey," Wapoose said. "I have one more lap to go."

"But there is no need," Buffalo said.

"But there is much I have not seen or learned," Wapoose said. "It is in the journey that one comes to understand the territory. It is in the journey that one becomes wise and I have one more lap to go."

They watched her disappear and after they had drank their fill and rested, they stood at the break in the trees and waited while Wapoose completed her trek around the lake. When she returned, they welcomed her. Eagle scooped her up in his strong talons and placed her on Buffalo's back, and together they walked back to the Animal People bearing a great story and a great teaching.

What Inspired Me to Write This Selection

"This story came from a desire to bring the traditional oral form to a contemporary setting and audience. I wanted to write a story that reflected the teaching tales of my people. I wanted to show that our traditions are alive and well, while entertaining people at the same time."

After

1. **Metacognition** Reread the story, paying attention to the timeline you created. How did rereading the story, with the aid of a timeline, help you to understand the story better?
2. **Critical Literacy** This story is told from the point of view of a third-person narrator.
   a) How does this point of view affect the way the story is told?
   b) How would the story be different if it was told from the point of view of Wapoose?
3. **Reading for Meaning** Wapoose says, "It is in the journey that one comes to understand the territory. It is in the journey that one becomes wise ...."
   a) What are other insightful statements made by Wapoose in this story?
   b) Which statement do you like the most? Why?
4. **Student Voice** How does your view of leadership compare to the one presented in the story?

Beyond

Listening and Speaking Create a soundscape or music list to accompany an oral retelling of this story. Present the story orally with your soundscape or music list.

Protect Our Land: A Youth Perspective

Personal Account

Originally published by SEVEN Youth Media

Written by Darryl Sainnawap

Darryl Sainnawap is 25 years old and serves as a youth councillor for Kitchenuhmaykoosib Inninuwug (KI), a First Nations community in northern Ontario. Sainnawap was one of six KI members sentenced to six months imprisonment for standing up against a mining company. He is a father of two beautiful, outgoing children, and soon to be married.

Tip

treaty: a legal agreement between the government of Canada and a First Nation that defines their relationship and establishes rights to land and other resources

Before

Make a list of things that you would fight to protect. Explain briefly why these things are worth fighting for.

During

1. As you read these two selections, think about what else you would like to know about Kitchenuhmaykoosib Inninuwug (KI), the government, and the mining company, Platinex.
2. As you read these selections, create a timeline of the events in the conflict between the leaders of KI and Platinex.

My name is Darryl Sainnawap. My spirit name is *Wichitaso Muskwa* (Helping Bear) as was given to me in a sweat lodge ceremony. I serve as the youth councillor for Kitchenuhmaykoosib Inninuwug (KI).

I would like to take this opportunity to share our story about KI's struggle to preserve our traditional lands and the journey we have travelled as a community. Our community has been in a dispute with the government of Ontario and an exploration company named Platinex. Our community has faced a $10 billion lawsuit, threats of bankruptcy, and the incarceration of the KI chief and council.

In January 2006, shortly after I was elected to council, an elder came into the boardroom and raised concerns about a company disturbing and interrupting his trapline. Workers for the company were cutting brush and doing other work that disturbed the animals and hurt the land. The company was Platinex.

The community leadership began sending letters to Platinex because we knew the company had been drilling for minerals on our traditional lands. The letters said Platinex was to halt work immediately. But it didn't.

February 2006—Platinex had a crew ready to get its big drilling equipment onto the land by using the winter roads. KI responded with a peaceful protest. By peaceful, we meant no guns, weapons, or violence would be tolerated at the protest. The Ontario Provincial Police (OPP) were present throughout the protest. After we spent three days protesting, drinking tea, and socializing with the drillers and OPP officers, Platinex finally decided to abandon its plans to drill and left.

April 2006—The community was served with court papers informing us that we were being sued for $10 billion! My first thought was of the second *Austin Powers* movie when Doctor Evil asks the president of the United States for $100 billion in the 1960s. The president laughs hysterically and mocks him: "I want a kajillion, bajillion dollars."

June 2006—We first entered the courtroom in front of Justice Patrick Smith in Thunder Bay, Ontario. Our lawyers argued that Ontario's *Mining Act* was unconstitutional because it did not respect Aboriginal and treaty rights. Platinex argued the company would go bankrupt if drilling did not proceed. Platinex also said the land it staked was public land, and was obtained legally through the *Mining Act*, a 135-year-old piece of legislation that gives a prospector the right to stake claims on any lands in the Province of Ontario.

July 28, 2006—Justice Smith released his decision that the Province of Ontario failed in its duty to consult KI before granting permits to Platinex. Justice Smith recognized that "KI's connection to the land was the essence of its being." He also found that KI did not act illegally or improperly during the protest in February 2006, and that Platinex left no other option for KI but to confront the company at the drill site. Platinex was prohibited from drilling for five months.

During the five months, KI, Platinex, and the Province of Ontario were ordered to meet to try to develop an agreement about mineral exploration.

January 2007—After attempts failed to reach an agreement, Platinex decided to sue the Province of Ontario, specifically the Ministry of Northern Development and Mines. The ban on drilling was extended until April 2007.

April 2007—All parties appeared before Justice Smith again. The Province of Ontario argued that KI surrendered its rights to its traditional lands when it signed the treaty. It said KI had no rights to the land other than for hunting, fishing, and trapping.

May 2007—Justice Smith agreed with the Province's arguments and released his decision that KI had no veto over its traditional lands since it was surrendered in the treaty. In the court's view, we weren't allowed to say no to a mining company.

When that decision was announced to the community, disappointment was in the air. The chief and council were stuck between a court order and community direction. But the community did not waiver in its opposition to mining.

We told Platinex that if the company attempted to proceed with its drilling program, community members would confront the company. Chief Donny Morris, Deputy Chief Jack McKay, Joseph McKay, Mark Anderson, Wallace Moskotaywenene, John A. McKay, Edward Anderson, and Lyle Ostaman set up camp at the drilling site to prevent Platinex from entering the traditional lands. They all stayed at the site for more than twenty days.

December 2007—We were once again in front of Justice Smith to answer to the contempt of court motion by Platinex. We were said to be in contempt because we were trying to stop Platinex from drilling.

We told our lawyer not to defend the motion and to inform the court that KI would not give Platinex access to the proposed drill site. The choice was to pay a fine or go to jail. But we couldn't afford to pay fines because we'd already paid so much in court costs. We informed the court that we would prefer to go to jail rather than go against our community's direction.

March 17, 2008—I'll never forget the day of the sentencing.

KI supporters march along Red River Road in Thunder Bay, Ontario, on March 18, 2008, the day after six members of KI council were sentenced to six months in jail.

That morning Justice Smith stated that he understood the beliefs and principles we were trying to uphold, but he went on to say that "the system of justice and rule of law are paramount and must be protected at all costs. Simply put, there is a fine line that no segment of society can be allowed to cross."

Chief Donny Morris, Deputy Chief Jack McKay, Head Councillor Cecilia Begg, Councillors Sam McKay, Bruce Sakakeep, and I accepted the sentence.

What stands out in my memory is Justice Smith reading his disposition and the words "You are hereby each sentenced to six months in jail." At that moment, reality set in—I was going to jail. Many thoughts flooded my mind. To be honest, I was nervous as I didn't know how jail was going to be since I'd never been in custody.

Amidst all my thoughts, I told myself that I would not compromise our people's direction. I told myself that I had an oath to uphold our land and our people. My oath as a councillor states that I have to "accept the guidance of our Creator and abide by the traditional values of our people, such as our role of being stewards of the land."

I knew we all missed our homes and families but we did what we believed in our hearts was right. We served 68 days of the 184-day sentence and were released on May 28, 2008.

Over the year since our release, we still hold the position of no drilling on our traditional lands. We have initiated negotiations with the Province of Ontario in the hopes that one day we will be an equal partner on our own land.

What Inspired Me to Write This Selection

"I felt compelled to share with my peers, and society in general, the reasons that Kitchenuhmaykoosib Inninuwug took a stand to preserve our pristine lands and waters. I felt it was important to share the events that transpired between KI and Platinex because I believe everyone in society could gain an understanding of First Nation values and learn from the unfortunate events of the struggle."

Now read "Protect Our Land: A Chief's Perspective" beginning on the next page.

Protect Our Land: A Chief's Perspective

Article

Written by Joyce Atcheson

Joyce Atcheson is a Métis journalist currently living in Dartmouth, Nova Scotia. She lived in Kitchenuhmaykoosib Inninuwug (KI) during some of the turmoil over mining, and supported the community in its court battles in Thunder Bay.

Tip

square brackets [ ]: square brackets are sometimes used to clarify information in direct quotations. Joyce Atcheson uses square brackets in some of the quotations from Chief Donny Morris in her article.

How many community leaders—mayors, premiers, or prime ministers—are forced to strip naked in front of two guards and spend sixty-eight days in jail for doing what the people who elected them told them to do?

That's what happened to Kitchenuhmaykoosib Inninuwug (KI) Chief Donny Morris.

"I was humiliated," Morris says of his March 2008 experience. He led peaceful protests against a mining company after a court order gave it the right to use

Councillor Bruce Sakakeep, Councillor Darryl Sainnawap, Councillor Samuel McKay, Chief Donny Morris, and Deputy Chief Jack McKay shortly after being sentenced to six months in prison for contempt of court charges.

land near KI. Community members asked their chief to protect the land that people traditionally use for hunting, fishing, and trapping. Morris, the deputy chief, and four councillors were subsequently sentenced to six months in jail on contempt of court charges.

Stripped and standing naked before two guards, Morris waited to be given the regulation orange coverall and wondered, "What will this mean to me as a leader, to leadership of the community, and to my family?"

"I had no problem washing floors and cleaning while I was there, but I still feel stripped of my integrity. I hold the position of chief in high regard. I was humiliated on behalf of the community. They [government, courts, and mining company] took this low way to expose us as criminals. Our intention was to uphold the community's position [to protect the land]. I lost my right to provide for my family, to be on the land in the spring hunt, to do as I am to do as a man."

Morris's commitment to leadership started in 1991 when two (late) elder, bedridden women, Rebecca Chapman and Juliette McKay, asked him to run for band council.

"They said, 'We will nominate you to run and if elected don't drink, don't do drugs, don't go to bars, and carry this job with the highest regard.' I never forget that. I couldn't say no to them. Sure enough, I was elected. I still cherish the concept of how to conduct myself as a leader. This lifestyle makes me see what I am to be. I'm not perfect as a chief or as a person, but I try to live to their expectations. I still hear my grandmother and those two elders scold me. One poked me with her cane as they told me what to do. It was not to be taken lightly," Morris says.

The land Morris stood to protect, known as Big Trout Lake, is a remote Oji-Cree First Nation of 1200 people, 750 km northwest of Thunder Bay, Ontario, north of what is shown on most road maps. This parent community of many surrounding First Nations is a fly-in community without sidewalks or pavement. Food; machinery; housing materials; vehicles; appliances; clothing; and fuel to generate electricity, heat homes, and power vehicles are delivered by air or transport truck. When cold weather permits, a winter road is built over the muskeg and links KI for a maximum of six weeks to the south. A plane ticket to Thunder Bay, the nearest city, costs about $1300.

But the land isn't out of reach to mining companies. Beginning in the 1990s, they expressed interest in KI's traditional lands and Morris says the people of KI repeatedly said no, telling their chief to protect the land, as their gift from the Creator.

"Not ready to jeopardize our future through unclear agreements, we knew we require unpolluted land for daily survival, given our cost of living. Our link to the land provides food, water, warmth, and shelter. I got my marching orders: I was told to 'Conduct peaceful protests to prevent intrusion by mining companies.'

"Our actions started when a trapper found shacks and men on the land. That's when the deputy [chief] and I went and told [the company men] they were 'not approved, not accepted, please leave.' The deputy and I stayed out there. We barred any violence, tire burning, flags, army fatigues, or face coverings that would cause anyone to call us rabble-rousers. We wanted everyone to know we are not militant and to show how important the land and the water are to our traditional life.

"We [Morris and a few men] used the land as we always do—hunting, fishing, trapping, snaring, making meals, and of course drinking tea as we shared stories. Children, youth, elders, women, and supporters from surrounding communities arrived to participate. We told them if we needed to, we would blockade the winter road and disrupt the ice runway the company had built to ferry their supplies.

"After that first time we knew when the company was coming, so we'd plan by getting our food ahead of time, hunting and fishing so we could live. The day before the company arrived, I'd take the guns from camp to hide them so no one could take up a gun and there would be no violence.

"Each time we protested [a total of three times] people came out to support us. Each protest lasted from five to twenty-one days. In the spring we only had one fishing boat out there, a 12-foot aluminum, with a 9 hp motor. Trolling, I kept the float plane from landing.

"Police came, but we were not there to hurt or harm anyone. We were there to protect our land. We had support from all over the world: South Africa, South America, the United States, England, Israel, Palestine, and Asian countries. We used the Internet and YouTube to cry for help, and, of course, we used prayer.

"After the court said we had to let them in, we met company executives at the airport. I think almost the whole community came out. We were packed like sardines in that building," Morris laughs as he talks.

KI's court experience began in 2006 when Platinex launched a $10 billion lawsuit against KI for denying the company access to the land. Ontario's laws, including the *Mining Act*, allow mining companies to dig and drill in a search for minerals against the wishes of the people who live nearby. But even before mining companies find minerals, there are laws that allow them to make money from their claims. They can sell shares in their company on the stock exchange or sell leases to the land on which they have staked claims. None of the money has to be shared with the nearby First Nation, even if the people there use the land for hunting and fishing and have their own claims to ownership.

KI was dragged into a court battle to argue for the right to say no to mineral exploration. But the provincial government told the courts that KI gave up its rights to its traditional lands when it signed a treaty with Canada and Ontario in 1929. KI doesn't agree with that view of the treaty, and those issues remain unresolved. The court battle dragged on and soon lawyer fees and associated costs depleted KI's finances. Money for fines for going against the court's orders did not exist and KI's leaders placed themselves at the mercy of the courts. The mining company and government lawyers demanded jail time to uphold the court's jurisdiction.

Knowing what he knows now and how this played out, Morris says he would do it again.

"The hardest part was the years of court, to keep it all together and move forward. It was harder than going to jail.

"This is about exploitation of our resources without our community getting what we need to bring us up to par. The treaty was signed in KI. And Canada, as our treaty partner, didn't come to our aid. Ontario, our other treaty partner, was the reason we were jailed. I would have wanted a commission party to revamp the *Mining Act* but we were excluded. We need to be self-governing, self-sufficient, and have jurisdiction over our land that Canada and Ontario claim. Most of all I'd like to protect my language and culture."

Chief Morris wanted to pass this message along to young people reading his story: "You and me are treaty partners and we have an obligation to fulfill that treaty, to make a better world for ourselves. My people don't have that. First Nations schools get $6000 per kid [from the federal government], but other schools in Canada [are provincially funded and] get $17 000 per child. We want equality with the treaty partners. I encourage you to finish school. You are our future leaders. When we say that here we mean it."

After

1. **Reading for Meaning** Why were the leaders of KI put in jail? Choose the best answer from the choices below.
   A. They held violent protests against the mining company.
   B. They were in contempt of court for trying to stop the mining company from drilling.
   C. They were trespassing on land that belonged to the mining company.
   D. They had enough money to pay the fines they owed, but thought it would make more of a statement if they went to jail.
2. **Reading for Meaning** How do these two perspectives—from the youth councillor and the chief— complement each other? Do they present different versions of events?
3. **Critical Literacy** Whose voices are missing from these selections? What do you think they would say if their voices were included?
4. **Reading for Meaning** Chief Morris is quoted as taking steps to ensure protests would be nonviolent. How does the image of protesters drinking tea and socializing with Platinex workers compare to other protests you have heard about? What does this tell you about the people of KI?
5. **Reading for Meaning** Chief Morris talks about being humiliated and treated as a criminal. The author suggests that municipal, provincial, and federal leaders would not be treated in such a manner. What does this comment suggest about First Nations–government relations?
6. **Student Voice** In your opinion, do you think that the chief and councillors were unlawfully confined in jail? Explain your answer.
7. **Metacognition** Were there any words in the articles that you were unfamiliar with? If so, what strategies did you use to understand their meaning?

Beyond

Reading for Meaning Two views of justice are posed in the personal account by Darryl Sainnawap:

- Justice Smith states, "the system of justice and rule of law are paramount and must be protected at all costs. Simply put, there is a fine line that no segment of society can be allowed to cross."
- Darryl Sainnawap states, "My oath as a councillor states that I have to 'accept the guidance of our Creator and abide by the traditional values of our people, such as our role of being stewards of the land.'"

a) What is in opposition in these two statements? Find support in the selections for your answer.
b) Imagine and construct a scenario where KI, the mining company, and the government could come to an agreement. Present your scenario as a short courtroom drama or written court decision.

Changes in the Indian Act

Graphic Art

By Chris Bose

Chris Bose is of the N'laka'pamux/Secwepemc Nations in British Columbia. He is a writer, multidisciplinary artist, musician, and filmmaker. He also facilitates workshops on art and digital storytelling. He currently spends his time in Kelowna and Kamloops, British Columbia.

Tips

Indian Act: a set of laws first passed by the Canadian government in 1876 and still enforced today, although the act has undergone many changes. It regulates the relationship between First Nations peoples and Canada, including government, education, health services, land, tax, and legal matters.

basketry: an important social and cultural activity in First Nations culture, during which the history of the people was discussed. These baskets usually contained survival items, such as food and medicine.

Before

Define the term *rights*. Brainstorm examples of rights you and your classmates currently have and take advantage of.

During

As you view this image, think about the rights that First Nations peoples were denied before 1951. Why is this important to know?

What Inspired Me to Create This Selection

"I was inspired by an overwhelming urge to create awareness of the struggle we go through as First Nations people. Historical acts still impact heavily on the reality of our modern world. I wanted to comment on how little this is noticed by anyone besides us. If we forget the past, we are doomed to repeat the same mistakes."

After

1. **Reading for Meaning** The woman in this photograph is preparing materials to make baskets. Why do you think the artist used basketry as a visual metaphor in this selection? Use the information from the Tip on this page for help. Do you think this metaphor is effective in communicating meaning?
2. **Reading for Meaning** What issues can you identify in this graphic art surrounding race, class, and power relations? Explain.
3. **Critical Literacy** Predict the responses that this graphic art would get from a First Nations person, a non-Aboriginal person, and a politician or government official in 1951 and today.

4. **Understanding Form and Style** How does this media form shape the message of the selection? Does it communicate meaning in an effective way? Why or why not?
5. **Metacognition** What are the similarities and differences between this selection and others like it that you have analyzed in this anthology?
6. **Student Voice** Has your understanding of the history of First Nations peoples changed after studying this selection? If so, how has it changed?

Beyond

Reading for Meaning Research changes made to the *Indian Act* since 1960. What are some of the most significant changes? In a form of your choice, present your findings on how the *Indian Act* limited and continues to limit the activities of First Nations peoples. Include information on how the *Indian Act* affects Inuit and Métis peoples.

UNTITLED

Photograph

Photographed by Nadya Kwandibens

Nadya Kwandibens is Ojibway (Anishinaabe) and French from the Northwest Angle #37 First Nation in Ontario. Identifying with her Ojibway heritage, she is also known as Makoons and is from the Loon Clan. She is a self-taught photographer specializing in artistic natural-light portraiture and event photography. Her work has appeared in various magazines such as *This*, *Spirit*, *SAY*, and *Red Ink*. She founded Red Works Studio, a photography company that empowers contemporary Indigenous lifestyles and cultures through photographic essays, features, and portraits.

Before

This photo is currently untitled. Give it a title. Why did you give it this title?

During

As you view the photo, what questions do you have for the photographer?

What Inspired Me to Create This Selection

"We, as Indigenous people, are often portrayed in history books as nations once great; in museums as nations frozen stoic; in the media as nations forever troubled. These images can be despairing; however, my goal seeks to steer the positive course. If our history is a shadow, let this moment serve as light. We are musicians, lawyers, doctors, mothers, and sons. We are activists, scholars, dreamers, fathers, and daughters. Let us claim ourselves now and see that we are, and will always be, great, thriving, balanced civilizations capable of carrying ourselves into that bright new day."

After

1. **Reading for Meaning** What main theme is expressed in this photo? Are other themes presented?
2. **Critical Literacy** Do you think the photographer assumes the viewer holds certain values or views of the world? What might those assumptions be?
3. **Reading for Meaning** What effect does the young woman looking at the camera have in this photo? How does this connect to the photographer's statement of inspiration?
4. **Understanding Form and Style** How would you describe the style of this photo? How effective is it in conveying the meaning of the photo?

5. **Student Voice** Look back at the title you gave this photo. After reading the photographer's inspiration and analyzing the photo, do you still think your title is appropriate or would you give it a new one?
6. **Metacognition** How does knowing why the photographer took this photo help you understand it?

Beyond

Student Voice Select an issue that is important to you. Take a photo that represents that issue. Explain orally or in writing how the photo relates to your views on the issue.

Mystery Girl

Poetry

Written by Louise B. Halfe – Sky Dancer

Louise B. Halfe–Sky Dancer was raised on the Saddle Lake Reserve in Alberta. Beyond her family's control, Louise and her siblings were transferred to a residential school. In addition to being a poet, Louise has a Bachelor of Social Work with a subspecialty in addictions counselling. Her books have received numerous accolades and awards, and she served as Saskatchewan's Poet Laureate for two years.

Before

Construct a web with the title "Mystery Girl" at the centre. Brainstorm your ideas and thoughts about the title.

During

As you read this poem, make new notes about what is meant by the title "Mystery Girl."

Tips

sweat lodge: a structure used to induce sweating for medicinal or spiritual purposes

sun dance: a spiritual ceremony practised among First Nations peoples, marked by several days of fasting and group dancing

medicine man: a person who acts as a bridge between the natural and spirit world, and seeks help from the spirit world for healing, divination, and control over natural events

I am the daughter
of a woman who was raised
in boarding school.
She was the daughter of
a woman raised in a convent.

I am the granddaughter
of woman who ran a sweat lodge
underneath a table. She used roots, herbs,
bones, and skins.

I am the niece of an auntie
who runs the lodge naked.
She throws sticks in the night
dark voices walk with her.

I am the little sister of a woman
who was beaten by my mother,
abused by my father,
and became a rag doll
for her husband.

I am the aunt of a woman
who came into my life as my little sister.
She sun danced until I pulled the pegs
off her arms.

I am the mother
of a little woman who has fasted
year after year
since the moon entered her body.

I am the grandmother
of two, one who skates
like Bobby Orr
and one who swims like a dolphin.

I am the wife of a medicine man
the mother of a medicine man
the mother of a doctor.
I am a sister, an aunt, a flower,
a thorn, a fire, a storm.

I am Mystery.

Buffalo Woman by Aaron Paquette

What Inspired Me to Write This Selection

"I wrote "Mystery Girl" when I thought about the complexity of my life and I looked at the many women I've observed growing up. I thought about this complex yet simple and down-to-earth creature that I am."

After

1. **Metacognition** Reread the poem. Did rereading the poem enhance your understanding of it? If so, how?
2. **Reading for Meaning** Create a family tree of all the family members the poet mentions in this poem. Provide a short description of each family member based on what you have learned in the poem.
3. **Critical Literacy**
   a) Why do you think the poet chose to include the family members she mentions?
   b) What other family members might she have left out? Why might she have done that?
4. **Understanding Form and Style** What effect does the phrase "I am" at the beginning of each stanza have?

Beyond

Student Voice Create your own poem, rap, song lyrics, or collage using the words "I am."

Culture by Design

Autobiography

Written by Ronald Everett Green

Ronald Everett Green was born in Lax Kw'alaams, British Columbia, and is from the Killer Whale Clan on his mother's side. He is a fashion designer who seeks to incorporate the traditions of his culture into his contemporary designs.

Tips

totem poles: monumental sculptures carved from large trees, usually western red cedar, by First Nations peoples of the Pacific Northwest Coast of North America

whale breaching: a whale leaping out of water

Before

Look at the photographs of Ronald Everett Green's fashion designs. How do you think the title of this selection relates to these designs?

During

As you read, think about questions that you would like to ask the author regarding his journey in the fashion industry.

Imagine finding a job where you can stitch together everything that's important to you. I've managed to seamlessly establish a career that does just that. I am a businessman and an artist; a historian and a futurist; a technical expert and a storyteller. I weave the history and traditions of my people into the modern world. My full name is Ronald Everett Green and I am a fashion designer.

I first fell in love with making art while attending high school in Prince Rupert, British Columbia. I even sold a piece of artwork when I was in high school. But my training as a creative person began when I was a child.

I spent my early childhood in Lax Kw'alaams, or Port Simpson to the English. Even as I write this, you can get there only by boat or by plane. My mother was of the Killer Whale Clan and I inherit this from her. My earliest works are reflective of more traditional icons, made in blanket-work and screens, and as I acquired new skills, I translated these into fashion designs.

I've always been fascinated by the use of images and natural items, like cedar, in the fabrication of ceremonial clothing. Robes, blankets, and shawls were used during important ceremonies such as the raising of a totem pole. They were adorned with images of the clans and used shells, cedar, and sometimes copper. I seek to create a contemporary interpretation of these in my designs.

At the University of Victoria, I studied the history of trade blankets, how cedar bark capes were made, and many other techniques traditional to my culture. I created blanket-work with images of my childhood, using shell buttons, beads, and Melton wool. I experimented with other techniques such as batik and other fabric not usual to my traditional roots, and I developed my own style for these images. I am proud to say many of these items adorn galleries and resorts across Canada and the United States.

I'm inspired by the natural world: a whale breaching, an eagle soaring, a salmon fishing run. I also find inspiration in other artists who have created their own interpretations of their First Nations cultures such as Bill Reid, Darcy Moses, Norval Morrisseau, and many others.

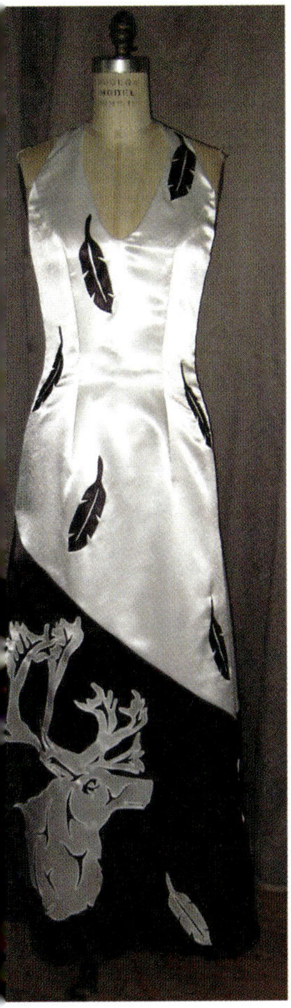

In the early 1990s, I moved to Toronto, where I was able to attend a fashion design program that provided me with the skills to incorporate my images of Killer Whale, Raven, and Wolf into fashion pieces. My goal is to integrate my culture with the design of a garment in a contemporary manner.

When I create my designs, the greatest inspiration comes from the person who commissions the piece. I want all the elements of the person who wears my clothes to come together in the piece, just as all aspects of my identity are expressed through the work I do. Who is that person? What images reflect his personality? Is she a teacher, like Wolf; or a trickster like Raven? Which silhouette complements her shape? All these forces come together to assist me in the design of the perfect piece, which reflects the personality and image of the wearer. Even for noncommissioned work, I consider the identity of someone who might buy the piece.

I am proud to list many Aboriginal and non-Aboriginal people in my client list. It is my intention to share my culture and my interpretation with all who wish to receive it.

After

1. **Reading for Meaning** The author refers to himself as a storyteller. Explain how he could be considered a storyteller.
2. **Reading for Meaning** Look at the photographs of the author's designs. What do you think the images in the designs (such as the eagle) are symbolizing? Why do you think the author has chosen these particular images?
3. **Critical Literacy** How do you think the author determines what kind of person he is creating designs for? What does this say about the author?
4. **Critical Literacy** How would the author's designs differ for his customers?
5. **Metacognition** Refer back to the questions that you would have liked to ask the author. Which ones were answered as you continued reading? How could you find out the answers to those that were not answered?

Beyond

1. **Reading for Meaning** Research the steps required for someone to go into the fashion design industry. Provide a step-by-step outline.
2. **Student Voice** Research the characteristics of animals in a First Nations culture. Choose an animal that you think best represents you. Design a piece of clothing that incorporates some aspect of that animal. Explain how this piece of clothing connects to your personality.

Dibenimiisowin [To Own Ourselves]

Speech and Essay

Written by Niigonwedom James Sinclair

Niigonwedom James Sinclair's essays and short stories have been translated into several languages and can be found in many journals, newspapers, and anthologies. Originally from St. Peter's (Little Peguis) First Nation in Manitoba, he now lives in Winnipeg, Manitoba.

Before

What do you know about Indian residential schools in Canada? Why were residential schools created?

During

As you read the statement of apology, pay close attention to the language used by the prime minister. What impact does this language have on the author's response to the apology?

Tips

***mishom*:** short form for *mishomis* which means grandfather [in the Ojibway language]

dash (—): longer than a hyphen, can be used like commas or parentheses to set off a parenthetical remark or aside. Dashes sometimes set off text that the author wants to emphasize.

Excerpts from Prime Minister Stephen Harper's Statement of Apology on June 11, 2008

I stand before you today to offer an apology to former students of Indian residential schools. The treatment of children in Indian residential schools is a sad chapter in our history.

In the 1870's, the federal government, partly in order to meet its obligation to educate Aboriginal children, began to play a role in the development and administration of these schools.

Two primary objectives of the residential schools system were to remove and isolate children from the influence of their homes, families, traditions and cultures, and to assimilate them into the dominant culture.

These objectives were based on the assumption Aboriginal cultures and spiritual beliefs were inferior and unequal.

Indeed, some sought, as it was infamously said, "to kill the Indian in the child."

Today, we recognize that this policy of assimilation was wrong, has caused great harm, and has no place in our country.

Most schools were operated as "joint ventures" with Anglican, Catholic, Presbyterian or United churches.

The government of Canada built an educational system in which very young children were often forcibly removed from their homes, often taken far from their communities.

Many were inadequately fed, clothed and housed.

All were deprived of the care and nurturing of their parents, grandparents and communities.

First Nations, Inuit and Métis languages and cultural practices were prohibited in these schools.

Tragically, some of these children died while attending residential schools and others never returned home.

The government now recognizes that the consequences of the Indian residential schools policy were profoundly negative and that this policy has had a lasting and damaging impact on Aboriginal culture, heritage and language.

While some former students have spoken positively about their experiences at residential schools, these stories are far overshadowed by tragic accounts of the emotional, physical and sexual abuse and neglect of helpless children, and their separation from powerless families and communities.

The legacy of Indian residential schools has contributed to social problems that continue to exist in many communities today. It has taken extraordinary courage for the thousands of survivors that have come forward to speak publicly about the abuse they suffered.

It is a testament to their resilience as individuals and to the strength of their cultures.

Regrettably, many former students are not with us today and died never having received a full apology from the government of Canada.

Prime Minister Stephen Harper delivers the Statement of Apology on June 11, 2008, in the House of Commons. Assembly of First Nations Chief Phil Fontaine (in headdress) listens as the speech is delivered.

The government recognizes that the absence of an apology has been an impediment to healing and reconciliation.

Therefore, on behalf of the government of Canada and all Canadians, I stand before you, in this chamber so central to our life as a country, to apologize to Aboriginal peoples for Canada's role in the Indian residential schools system.

To the approximately 80,000 living former students, and all family members and communities, the government of Canada now recognizes that it was wrong to forcibly remove children from their homes and we apologize for having done this.

We now recognize that it was wrong to separate children from rich and vibrant cultures and traditions, that it created a void in many lives and communities, and we apologize for having done this.

We now recognize that, in separating children from their families, we undermined the ability of many to adequately parent their own children and sowed the seeds for generations to follow, and we apologize for having done this.

We now recognize that, far too often, these institutions gave rise to abuse or neglect and were inadequately controlled, and we apologize for failing to protect you.

Not only did you suffer these abuses as children, but as you became parents, you were powerless to protect your own children from suffering the same experience, and for this we are sorry.

The burden of this experience has been on your shoulders for far too long.

The burden is properly ours as a government, and as a country.

There is no place in Canada for the attitudes that inspired the Indian residential schools system to ever again prevail.

You have been working on recovering from this experience for a long time and in a very real sense, we are now joining you on this journey.

The government of Canada sincerely apologizes and asks the forgiveness of the Aboriginal peoples of this country for failing them so profoundly.

We are sorry.

In moving towards healing, reconciliation and resolution of the sad legacy of Indian residential schools, implementation of the Indian Residential Schools Settlement agreement began on September 19, 2007.

Years of work by survivors, communities, and Aboriginal organizations culminated in an agreement that gives us a new beginning and an opportunity to move forward together in partnership.

A cornerstone of the settlement agreement is the Indian Residential Schools Truth and Reconciliation Commission.

This commission presents a unique opportunity to educate all Canadians on the Indian residential schools system.

It will be a positive step in forging a new relationship between Aboriginal peoples and other Canadians, a relationship based on the knowledge of our shared history, a respect for each other and a desire to move forward together with a renewed understanding that strong families, strong communities and vibrant cultures and traditions will contribute to a stronger Canada for all of us.

Dibenimiisowin [To Own Ourselves]

A version of this essay originally appeared in *Urban NDN* (July 2008).

Two events defined my June 11, 2008.

The first came at 2 PM, when I watched and listened with anticipation, anxiety, and anger as the prime minister of Canada apologized for the institution and legacy of the residential school system. During those next few hours I, like many, recounted the numerous traumas embedded in the histories of our communities, our families, and our people.

I thought of the experiences of my family, my partner's family, and countless parents, uncles, aunties, and friends. I thought of what happened years later, in both their own and their children's lives. I thought of what my cousins and I live with today.

I thought of our leaders who, although far from perfect, bravely fought to get what National Chief Phil Fontaine called "the achievement of the impossible." I thought of some of our non-Native allies, who fought alongside Indigenous peoples, even as these contributions are hardly ever known.

I thought about how for many—including myself—the apology was an historic opportunity and a chance, perhaps a small one, at a new future. I thought about how, for some, it would not be acceptable. I thought about how both views are right.

I thought about the racism that went into these schools, the arrogance that justified abusing children, and the

Residential school survivor Connie Brooks reacts during a Letting Go ceremony at the site of the Shubenacadie Residential School in Nova Scotia on June 11, 2008.

shadow of white privilege that stretches into today—evident even in the very space where the ceremony took place. The House of Commons is the place, after all, where French and English continue to be privileged (and supported) as the "founding" nations, languages, and cultures of Canada. It is also the place where a department of "Indian Affairs" enforces "legislative authority" over "Indians, and Lands reserved for the Indians" (*BNA Act*, Sec. 91). It is also the place that for years refused to ratify the United Nations Declaration on the Rights of Indigenous Peoples, which includes (among other things) basic protections against cultural and political assimilation as well as an acknowledgement of the "collective right to live in freedom, peace and security as distinct peoples and ... not be subjected to any act of genocide or any other act of violence, including forcibly removing children of the group to another group." And let's not forget, it took 141 years (the entire time Canada has been a nation) for Native leaders to speak in the House of Commons "officially" to Canadians.

I thought about the infinite ways all lives, Native and non-Native, have been touched by residential school experiences.

And—for good or for bad—I shed more than a few tears during the apology.

Then, in the middle of my crying and remembering, my two-year-old came over to me and, with her little arms, grabbed me around the neck. "Dadadada," she said, refusing to let go. I held her right back.

She asked me why I was crying. Together we watched the rest of the speeches, and I tried telling her why. She seemed worried about me, so I told her we could go outside. Then we dug up some worms in the garden. It's her favourite thing to do. Afterward, my daughter and I went for a drive to get some ice cream. It was a warm afternoon and I thought we both deserved it.

Which leads me to the second event.

Coming up Main Street and reaching the intersection at Euclid Avenue (in the north end of Winnipeg), I saw him.

A man, passed out in the middle of the intersection. Dozens of cars passing by. His lady friend, trying to lift him up. Failing. Falling. The man, face down on the pavement.

More cars passing by. One vehicle, passing through the intersection, slowly drove around him. It was like he wasn't there, but he was—if that makes any sense.

Without really thinking, I stopped, got out, and locked our van. Right in the middle of traffic.

"Are you all right?" I asked the man.

A black truck slowed down to watch us, before speeding away down the street.

It was an old Native man—looked in his sixties. Probably somebody's *mishom*. Maybe even a relative.

I couldn't help but think, particularly in the context of the day, that this was likely a residential school survivor. He certainly reminded me of my grandfather.

By this time, eight cars had stopped behind our van, creating quite a little jam. None of them honked, told me to move, or cursed at me. None of them got out to help, either. They just sat there. Through the windshield I could see my daughter, in her car seat, watching too.

The man tried to stand and speak. In the state he was in, both were difficult, so I helped him. Then, a young man—Native too, I think—ran out into the intersection to help. We put the elder's arms around our necks and walked him to a nearby bus stop bench. I gave the young man twenty bucks to go and buy the man something to eat. He came back three minutes later with Cokes and sandwiches.

Returning to our van, I opened the door and climbed inside.

"Dadadada," said my daughter, as we drove away.

Since then, I've thought lots about these two events. I've heard countless writers, reporters, and pundits debate the significance of the apology. I've heard one shortsighted writer claim that it was meant to give Native peoples healing.

No apology, no words, and certainly no time in Parliament, can give healing. No passing of any bill or law will do that either. Money, resources, and time might help, but none of these ultimately can do the job.

Healing is on all of us, as Indigenous peoples, to do ourselves. Others can help us—and this is important—but we can't wait for anyone else's "help." We can't wait for others to say sorry, to listen to our experiences, or to get out of their damn cars.

To attain healing, we have to be as brave as our children—who take the risk of loving us—no matter how complex we are or how many mistakes we make. We have to have the courage to bravely inherit our lives, our communities, and our nations by helping ourselves, even if this results in us digging up many worms.

Cultural Co-ordinator John Fox comforts a residential school survivor during a smudging cleansing ceremony in Toronto, Ontario, while Prime Minister Stephen Harper reads the Statement of Apology on television.

One opportunity to do this will be during the Truth and Reconciliation Commission, where we will have a chance to share our stories of residential schools and their legacies while listening to others in a spirit of compassion, respect, and honesty. It won't be easy. The past will be both beautiful and ugly, and sometimes both at the same time—that's all I know it will be.

But we must do so ourselves.

That's how you achieve the impossible.

What Inspired Me to Write This Selection

> "I wrote this piece reflecting on the irony I witnessed on the day of the apology for residential schools. It's about choices, the differing paths we've travelled as peoples and nations, and considers the distance we have yet to go. I also wrote it in the hope that my daughter would read it one day and realize how much she has taught me."

After

1. **Reading for Meaning** The author begins the essay by saying, "Two events defined my June 11, 2008."
   a) What are these two events?
   b) How does the author see the events relating to one another?
2. **Reading for Meaning** Why do you think the author chose the title "To Own Ourselves"? How does this title relate to the content of his essay?
3. **Critical Literacy** Describe at least one example from the essay that the author believes demonstrates racism. Explain why the author views this example as racist.
4. **Reading for Meaning**
   a) Why do you think these photos were chosen to accompany this essay?
   b) What do you think the people in the photos are thinking or feeling?
5. **Student Voice** In your opinion, do you think the prime minister's apology is enough to make up for what the survivors of residential schools experienced or lost? Explain.
6. **Metacognition** How does the information you read in the apology and the essay align with what you already know? Has it altered your views? Explain.

Beyond

Reading for Meaning Research a residential school survivor's personal story. Present your research in whatever form you like (such as an oral presentation, video, poem, or graphic story).

Truth and Reconciliation

Speech

By Justice Murray Sinclair

Justice Murray Sinclair was born and raised on St. Peter's Reserve in the Selkirk area north of Winnipeg, Manitoba. He graduated from his high school as class valedictorian and athlete of the year in 1968. After a successful career as a lawyer, he was appointed associate chief judge of the Provincial Court of Manitoba in 1988, and then to the Court of Queen's Bench of Manitoba in 2001. He was Manitoba's first judge of First Nations descent. He has been awarded a National Aboriginal Achievement award in addition to many other community service awards, as well as honourary degrees from the University of Manitoba, the University of Ottawa, and St. John's College (University of Manitoba). Justice Sinclair's Ojibway name is *Mizanay Gheezhik*, which means "the One Who Speaks of Pictures in the Sky."

Tips

residential schools: boarding schools run mainly from the 1830s to the 1950s to educate First Nations, Métis, and Inuit children and erase their traditional languages and cultures. Students were often forcibly removed from their homes and families and subjected to abuse in these schools.

treaty: a legal agreement between the government of Canada and a First Nation that defines their relationship and establishes rights to land and other resources

Before

What does respect mean to you? Do you think having self-respect is important? Why or why not?

During

As you read this speech, think about the tone and language Justice Sinclair is using. Who is the speech directed to? How is this evident?

This is an excerpt from a speech given by Justice Murray Sinclair, commissioner of Canada's Truth and Reconciliation Commission, at a community forum in Sioux Lookout, Ontario, in the spring of 2010.

The Truth and Reconciliation Commission was set up by the Canadian federal government to learn the truth about what happened in the residential schools and to inform all Canadians about the residential school system and its legacy. The intention of the Commission is to guide and inspire First Nations, Inuit, and Métis peoples and Canadians in a process of truth and healing, which, it is hoped, will lead toward reconciliation and renewed relationships based on mutual understanding and respect.

Reconciliation is about respect. It is about respect.

When the treaties were signed, those who signed the treaties on behalf of the First Nations people, their intent at that time was very clear. It's in all of the documentation on both sides of the debate. The intent was: we will share this land with you. We promise that we will get along with you. We promise that we will respect your right to be here and what we ask in return is you respect our right to be here.

It boils down to a conversation I had once with an elder, a survivor who was speaking at a gathering that occurred at Spanish, Ontario. And I said to him, what do you think reconciliation is? And he said, "Well, I'm not real sure, but I think reconciliation is if we can get the government to understand that they don't own this place and they should stop acting like they own this place."

That's reconciliation. Stop acting like you own the place and understand that we own it, too. But now we own it together. That's what he's talking about. That's what reconciliation is. Reconciliation is not the establishment of a new legal relationship. Reconciliation is about the establishment of the relationship that was intended and that relationship was a respectful one.

But before we can have that mutually respectful relationship, I think we have to have a preliminary step. And that is to our children, for our children, we have to give them self-respect. Our young people do not understand the validity of their own lives. Our young people do not know who they are. Our young people do not know their Creation story. They do not know the story of the life hereafter. They do not know their purpose in life and so they do not know who they are. We need to give that to them. We need to give them that sense of validity. We need to give them that sense of identity. We need to help them understand their responsibilities to each other and their responsibilities to Creation. If we do not do that, then they will continue down a path of self-destruction that we see reflected today in the suicide rates, in the self-abuse rates, in the addiction rates, in incarceration rates that are still rampant.

I was a commissioner of the Aboriginal justice inquiry in Manitoba in 1991. We reported that 77 percent of the young people locked up in the jails in Manitoba were Aboriginal youth. I can tell you now it's probably close to 90 percent. It's gone up. Why has it gone up? It's because even though we recognize the terrible things we're doing in the justice system, that's not where the solution lies. The solution lies in giving to our children, our young people, a better sense of their identity and of their responsibilities to each other.

Back in 1991 when we issued that report, young Aboriginal people were committing crimes largely against white people. They were defacing property, they were stealing property, they were attacking other young people in the schools. But since then the crime has turned inward. We now see more and more violence directed at other young Aboriginal people. The young people who are being murdered by Aboriginal people are not young white people. Aboriginal youth are killing other Aboriginal youth. It's because of the influence of gangs; it's the influence of other criminal elements that have given them that sense of direction. Because we can't give them that sense of direction, others are doing it for them. And we don't need that to happen. We need to do something about it.

It was education that got us to this point in time, an education system that was fundamentally flawed. And that was the residential school system. But despite that, the education system is what is going to get us out of this. We need to change the way we educate our children on both sides of the equation, our Aboriginal children, our non-Aboriginal children. We need to ensure that our education system has within it knowledge and information about the residential school legacy of this country. We need to ensure that all children are taught about the validity of Aboriginal people and their belief systems and who they are and where they come from. We need to ensure that Aboriginal heroes are showcased just as much as non-Aboriginal heroes are in our history books. We need to ensure that people like Tecumseh (who is a hero to the Ojibway people), that his story is told in our school system. We need to ensure that people like Big Bear and Poundmaker, and what they stood for in their part of the world, that that story is told.

We need to ensure that all of the stories of the First Nations people in this world are shared not just with the Aboriginal kids, but also with the non-Aboriginal kids because, you have to remember, and it's so fundamentally logical that it kind of escapes us: if we were teaching Indian kids that they were weak and inferior, then we were also teaching the white kids that. And I use that word [*Indian*] advisedly, incidentally. I'm not intending on offending anybody. But the education system was teaching both sets of children that very fundamental belief and that is that what is Indian is inferior, what is Aboriginal is inferior. So not only did our children, Aboriginal children, grow up with that belief, but non-Aboriginal children grew up with that belief as well, and it inadvertently gave them a false sense of superiority. And you know who I'm talking about,

Justice Sinclair speaks during a sharing circle that was part of the Truth and Reconciliation Commission.

I'm talking about you here in this room. You don't know it, but the people you went to school with grew up with a false sense of security. And what does that lead to? It leads to racism. It leads to racism in our words, our actions, our thoughts, and our deeds, in everything that we do, in our unconscious statements about things.

The prime minister of Canada, within a year of giving that wonderful apology (that wonderful heartfelt apology that moved all of us to tears), within a year of saying that, at an international conference not long afterwards, he said that Canada has no history of colonialism. And he meant that, he believed that. But, unconsciously he did not realize what he was saying. He couldn't have, because otherwise that apology means nothing. Because that apology was all about colonialism. That apology was all about the wrongness of the government to do what it believed against other people because of the inferiority of their race.

So we need to look at the way we educate our children. We need to ensure that our young people are given a sense of validity, that they know where they come from, they know where they're going, they know why they're here, then they'll know who they are. If we can address those things as objectives, as the purpose of reconciliation, and recognize that we're not going to achieve that in five years, that's ultimately going to be our objective. Then what we have to talk about is how we keep that in the forefront of our thinking. How do we keep that in the forefront of our thinking so that everything we do from now on is premised upon the intent, and the goal of respect, of mutual respect? That has got to be our goal.

After

1. **Reading for Meaning** In your own words, explain why Justice Sinclair views respect as being central to treaties between First Nations and the Canadian government.
2. **Reading for Meaning** What does Justice Sinclair think is important to teach all students?
3. **Critical Literacy** Do you think this speech reveals any biases that Justice Sinclair may have? Explain.
4. **Understanding Form and Style** What elements of this text make it clear that it is a speech?
5. **Metacognition** At what points in reading Justice Sinclair's speech did you stop to evaluate his views? Explain your conclusions.
6. **Student Voice** Explain what reconciliation means to you.

Beyond

Reading for Meaning Research a First Nations treaty in your province. Create a brief presentation, in a format of your choice, explaining the terms of the treaty and the responsibilities of both sides.

North

The People's Wisdom

BIG IDEA

Why is it important for wisdom to be passed on to future generations?

The North represents elements of winter, wisdom, the spiritual aspects of a person, and the elder phase of personal development.

In this final section of the anthology, First Nations, Inuit, and Métis peoples share in stories, images, and words their unique creativity and cultural wisdom. You will meet an Anishinabe rapper who shares his talent to expose current issues. You will learn about the authentic origins of cultural artifacts such as the dream catcher. You will laugh with a Dogrib family as they encounter an ancient being. And you will be mesmerized by the profound graphic pieces that tell their own story of struggle and strength.

The selections in North will help you recognize the truths within yourself, in others, and in the earth around you. Each of the writers offers us a reflective look at our heroes, teachers, adversaries, and elders. These selections will have you thinking about your own wisdom and the importance of sharing this with the world.

The Trial of Duncan C. Scott

Graphic Art

By Chris Bose

Chris Bose is of the N'laka'pamux/Secwepemc Nations in British Columbia. He is a writer, multidisciplinary artist, musician, and filmmaker. He also facilitates workshops on art and digital storytelling. He currently spends his time in Kelowna and Kamloops, British Columbia.

Tips

cultural genocide: the deliberate destruction of the cultural heritage of a people for political, military, religious, ideological, ethnic, or racial reasons

juxtaposition: the act of placing items or ideas side by side for comparison or contrast

Before

1. Before reading this selection, look over the images and predict whether the subject matter will be historical, contemporary, or both. Explain your thinking.
2. What do you know about the poet Duncan Campbell Scott and his role in Canadian history?

During

As you view this graphic art, think about the reasons the artist had for creating this piece. Why are they important to know?

Duncan Campbell Scott said the words quoted in this graphic art in 1920 when he was Deputy Superintendent of Indian Affairs in Canada. His policies led to the establishment of the Indian residential school system. The primary purpose of these schools was to forcefully "civilize" First Nations, Inuit, and Métis children. Children were taken to these boarding schools against their families' will, and they were often abused at these schools.

What Inspired Me to Create This Selection

"I was inspired by an overwhelming urge to create awareness of the struggle we go through as First Nations people. Historical acts still impact heavily on the reality of our modern world. I wanted to comment on how little this is noticed by anyone besides us. If we forget the past, we are doomed to repeat the same mistakes."

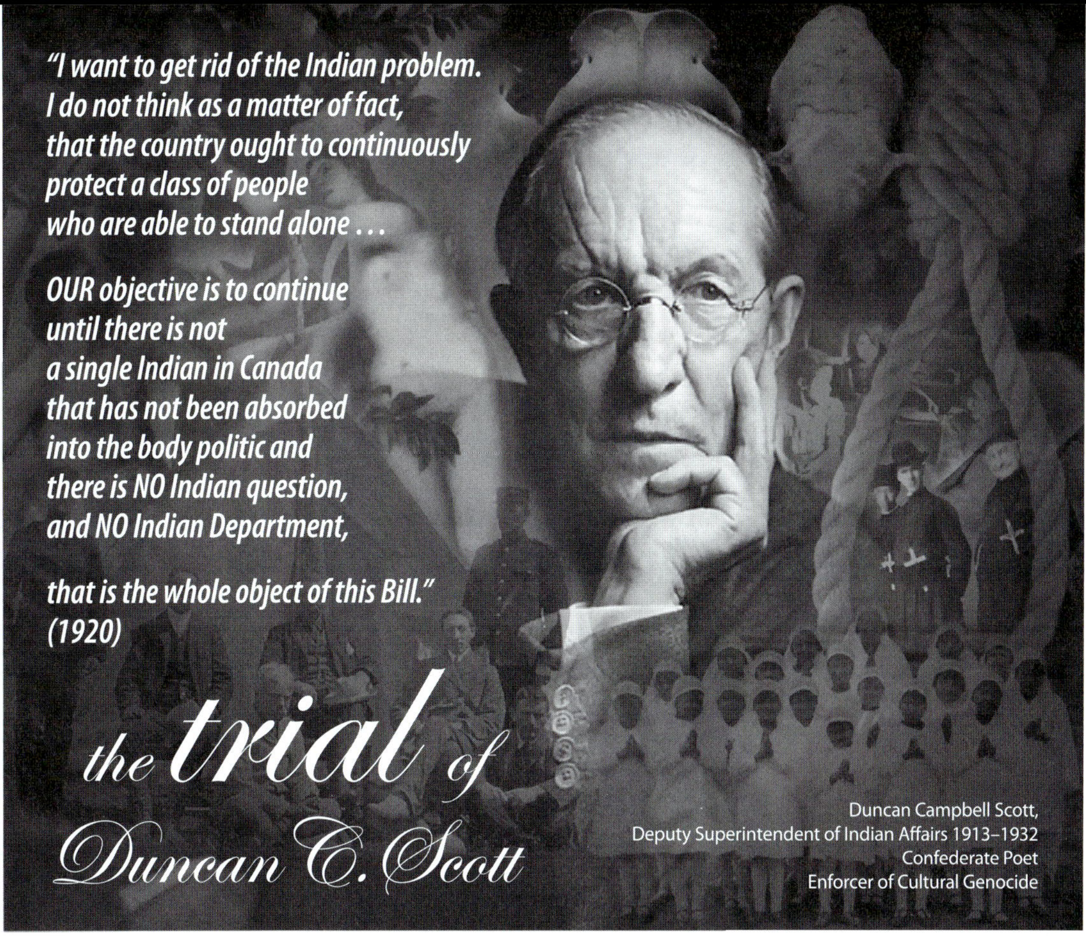

After

1. **Student Voice** What emotions did this selection evoke in you? Why do you think it had that effect on you?
2. **Reading for Meaning** Duncan Campbell Scott did not face a trial. Why do you think the artist chose the title "The Trial of Duncan C. Scott"?
3. **Understanding Form and Style**
   a) List the images that you see in this selection.
   b) How do the images reflect the meaning of the text?
   c) How does the juxtaposition of images help to create meaning in this selection?
4. **Critical Literacy** What is the artist trying to get us to believe about Duncan Campbell Scott? Explain your answer.
5. **Understanding Form and Style** Do you think this graphic art would have had a different impact if presented in colour, instead of black and white? Why or why not?
6. **Metacognition** Reflect on what you learned by reading and analyzing this selection. Why do you think it is important to reflect on your learning?

Beyond

Reading for Meaning Research other examples of cultural genocide around the world. Present your findings in a form of your choice, such as a collage, painting, sculpture, or written report. Explain how these examples are similar to and different from the cultural genocide experienced by First Nations, Inuit, and Métis peoples in Canada.

We Found Somebody

Burial site vindicates Ipperwash occupiers

Newspaper Article

Written by Maurice Switzer

Maurice Switzer is a citizen of the Mississaugas of Alderville First Nation, in southern Ontario. He wrote this article when he served as director of communications for the Union of Ontario Indians and editor of the *Anishinabek News*, where the article first appeared.

Tip

Ipperwash Provincial Park: The area formerly known as Ipperwash Provincial Park is located in southwestern Ontario on the eastern shore of Lake Huron. The province of Ontario has agreed to give the land back to Kettle and Stoney Point First Nation, but the transfer of land is still in process.

Before

Reflect on the title of this article. Predict possibilities for the content of this selection.

During

As you read, record the names of people mentioned in this article. Keep track of any information that you learn about these people.

STONEY POINT—Thousands of words were spoken during a commemorative gathering staged October 15, 2010 by members of Kettle and Stoney Point communities, but three words held special significance.

"We found somebody," said Brandy George, the only fully trained First Nation archeologist in Ontario. George told a hushed crowd seated in a striped tent, about 50 metres from where Dudley George was shot and killed on September 6, 1995, that her team had unearthed human remains in what was formerly Ipperwash Provincial Park.

Brandy, 36, a Kettle and Stoney Point citizen, said the burial site was determined to be at least 1000 years old, which pre-dates the arrival of Europeans in southwestern Ontario by more than three centuries.

"This is the greatest achievement in my life," she told the 200 people gathered to honour the 15th anniversary of Dudley George's death during an occupation of Ipperwash by a group of unarmed protesters.

"Pierre was with us [when we found the human remains]," Brandy said, standing beside Pierre George, the man who drove his fatally wounded brother to hospital the night he was shot by an Ontario Provincial Police sniper. "We offered tobacco and said the words we needed to say."

She said the discovery validates stories told by community elders that ancestors were buried in the area, a key motive for the occupation of the park by Stoney Point protesters 15 years earlier.

George said her exhaustive two-year study—digging holes every 5 metres—unearthed 11 archeological sites in the park in addition to the burial. Despite a previous assessment that the park had no archeological significance, George revealed that her project—funded by the province's Ministry of Aboriginal Affairs—produced artifacts dating back 8000 years.

"The artifacts will come back to the community," George said, stressing that they are in her personal care and being treated with appropriate respect.

George was introduced by Kettle and Stoney Point Chief Elizabeth Cloud, who wiped away tears as she told the gathering: "This shows that Dudley did not die in vain. The oral history of our elders is always true."

Brandy George (Photo courtesy of the *Anishinabek News*.)

Following the announcement guests left the tent, following flag and Eagle Staff carriers to the unveiling of a monument designed by Pierre George which read: "In Memory of Dudley George who made the Supreme Sacrifice September 6, 1995 In Respect of the Ancestors."

"This is an emotional time and a historic occasion," said Anishinabek Nation Grand Council Chief Patrick Madahbee. "Anishinaabe need to focus on Dudley's spirit of resistance and resolve to guide us. I will be proud to tell my grandchildren that I was there when a memorial was dedicated to a great warrior."

Madahbee commended Aboriginal Affairs Minister Chris Bentley for "trying to move the yardsticks" on Ipperwash-related issues, such as the drawn-out process to transfer the former provincial park to Kettle and Stoney Point reserve land. "Sometimes we need to get out of our canoe and into a speedboat."

Dudley George's siblings Caroline "Cully" George and Pierre George with Grand Council Chief Patrick Madahbee at the unveiling of the Dudley George monument in the former Ipperwash Provincial Park.
(Photo courtesy of the *Anishinabek News*.)

The Grand Council Chief recognized members of Dudley George's family, including his sister Caroline "Cully" George and brother Pierre who were among the Stoney Pointers who occupied the barracks at nearby Camp Ipperwash. Expropriated by Canada in 1942 for an army training camp, the land has yet to be transferred back to First Nation control.

Minister Bentley drew applause when he acknowledged being on the "soon-to-be-recognized traditional territory of the people of Kettle and Stoney Point," and the efforts of the late Sam George that led to the creation of the Ipperwash Inquiry into his brother Dudley's death.

Among those in attendance was Justice Sidney Linden, who served as commissioner for the two-year inquiry that produced 100 recommendations, including ones calling for establishment of a treaty commission in Ontario and better police training for dealing with First Nations people and issues.

An update on progress being made on responding to the recommendations was presented by First Nations Task Force participants in the Ipperwash Inquiry Priorities and Action Committee (IIPAC). Working groups were examining Ipperwash-related issues such as treaty rights, policing, burial sites, and public education. Task force members, including Union of Ontario Indians policy analyst Nicole Latulippe, fielded a number of questions from Kettle and Stoney Point community members.

The following day was dedicated to community healing, including a traditional condolence ceremony. Facilitators included Robert Antone, Oneida, director of a healing lodge in Muncey-Delaware First Nation, who acted as a mediator during the explosive 76-day standoff at Kahnesetake (Oka) in July, 1990.

"There have been struggles across the country over loss of land," said Antone. "Have governments learned anything from them? Could we have done anything differently here? Not from our side—it was a peaceful demonstration. It was the other side that used force. The resistance movement is not over; we're going to see it again."

What Inspired Me to Write This Selection

"There isn't a more important reason to create greater public awareness about First Nations issues than the fact that ignorance about these issues led to Dudley George's death."

After

1. **Metacognition**
   a) How did keeping track of the people mentioned in the article help you to make sense of the article?
   b) What other reading strategies might help you understand the article?
2. **Reading for Meaning** Explain why Brandy George's words, "We found somebody" were so significant.
3. **Critical Literacy** Do you think that the author empathizes with the Ipperwash protestors and Kettle and Stoney Point citizens? What elements of the article reveal his feelings?
4. **Student Voice** Do you think Brandy George's discovery vindicates the Stoney Point protestors' occupation of Ipperwash? Explain your thinking.
5. **Understanding Form and Style** This is an article from a newspaper. What other forms of media might have been used to present this same story? Which form of media do you think would be most effective? Why?

Beyond

1. **Reading for Meaning** Choose one person mentioned in the article whom you would like to know more about. Imagine you will interview that person and prepare a list of questions to ask.
2. **Reading for Meaning** Research the Ipperwash incident and the Dudley George inquiry. Present findings from your research in a form of your choice.

The Biggest Moccasins in the World

Short Story

Written by Richard Van Camp

Illustrated by Moses (Amik) Beaver

Richard Van Camp is a Dogrib (Tlicho) Dene from Fort Smith, Northwest Territories. He is an internationally known storyteller and best-selling author of adult and children's fiction. Richard was awarded Storyteller of the Year for both Canada and the United States by the Wordcraft Circle of Native Writers and Storytellers in 2007.

Tips

italics: words from other languages are set in italics; for example, *pardonnez-moi* and *mahsi cho.*

Dogrib: First Nations peoples who live in the Great Slave Lake area of the Northwest Territories

***Nagha* (Sasquatch):** a very large, hairy, humanlike creature said to live in remote wilderness areas of Canada and the United States

Old Man's Beard: a type of fungus with a hair-like appearance that grows on branches

***mahsi cho*:** thank you very much [in the Dogrib language]

Before

Do you know someone who tells good stories? What do you like about this person's storytelling? What makes a good story?

During

As you read this short story, think about what the author means when he says, "This is a story of respect from my family to you."

This is a story of respect from my family to you.

A long time ago when my mother, Rosa, was a little girl, she and her brothers and parents went hunting for caribou way up high on the barren lands. My grandpa, Pierre Washie, was a great hunter. He and other Dogrib men led many community hunts for years and always hunted to provide for people who couldn't hunt for themselves. My grandma, Melanie, was a superb cook. One of the many secrets to the success of her dry meat was that she bathed her caribou meat with the sweet smoke from diamond willows, seasoning it to make it the very best for her family and community.

My grandma was also an incredible moccasin maker. It's rumoured that the Queen herself buys my grandma's moccasins for all her buddies every Christmas. On New

Year's, they jig together to Métis fiddle music! The Queen is rumoured to be almost as good a jigger as my grandpa. Yes! The Queen and her pals get together and whoop it up all night long, just jigging away, boy, and dosey-do'ing—

(Ahem ahem ahem ... pardonnez moi!)

Well, back on the barren lands, as my mom, her two brothers, and my grandma and grandpa were sleeping, their dogs started to growl. Then they started to howl. Then they started to scream! It was scary to hear dogs screaming at something no one could see. So, without thinking, my uncle Eddie ran out of the tent to find out what was happening.

Well, he dabbed his nose into the cold nose of a Sasquatch! (In Dogrib, we call the Sasquatch the *Nagha* or Bushman.) Can you imagine who was more scared—my uncle or the *Nagha*?

My uncle said they were both scared. Touching noses, they yelled at each other as loud as they could. While everyone was screaming (even the dogs!), my grandpa fired his rifle into the air to scare away whatever it was that was causing all this excitement. Before the *Nagha* turned and ran, he tried to grab some of my grandma's famous dry meat from the smoke stand. But my grandpa was such a good carpenter that the *Nagha* couldn't knock the stand over, so he didn't get any dry meat at all.

It was then that my uncle Eddie got a good look at the *Nagha*. He stood and moved like a strong man, my uncle Eddie said, and he was huge, with long arms and powerful legs. He was covered in long hair, almost like Old Man's Beard, but softer. He had the face of a little boy but his eyes were big, like a moose. The *Nagha*'s hands were huge, like the hands of a man who has worked hard his whole life. His smell was strong, like burnt hair, making everyone's eyes water. (Can you believe my mom slept through all this?)

Well, my family got up and saw the tracks the *Nagha* had left. My uncle Eddie said the tracks were so huge that he could place a full litter of six baby huskies inside the track and they could all stretch out and wiggle their little toes as they yawned.

My grandma and grandpa started to break camp.

"How cheap! Why do we have to move?" Uncle Eddie asked. Now that the *Nagha* was gone, he was getting cheeky.

"All animals have trails," my grandpa explained. "We set up camp late and missed the signs that we were on the *Nagha*'s trail. The *Nagha* are shy people. He would not have bothered us if we hadn't set up camp in his territory."

My grandma took apart four pairs of moccasins that no one was using. She made one big pair for the footsteps the stranger had left behind.

"What are you doing?" Uncle Eddie asked.

"Making a gift for a new friend," she answered.

When my family moved camp, they left behind the dry meat the *Nagha* had tried to gather and a huge pair of moccasins as a way of saying they were sorry for trespassing on his territory.

My uncle Eddie said that a week later, when they were on their way home, they passed by the same spot and the dogs started to whimper. Uncle Eddie could see the fresh tracks of the *Nagha*. The dry meat they left behind was gone and so was the huge pair of my grandma's moccasins. The tracks leading up to the smoke stand were from bare feet, while the trail leading away was made with the biggest moccasined feet anyone had ever seen.

Can you believe that? My uncle Eddie told me that story one day in Fort Rae. He was getting ready to go fight fires and we were having tea.

"Yup," he said, "your grandma should be in the *Guinness World Records* for making the biggest pair of moccasins in human and *Nagha* history. And I should be in there too, for being the first Dogrib Indian to ever touch noses with a Sasquatch!"

Is this cool, or what? This is a true story! *Mahsi cho!*

What Inspired Me to Write This Selection

"This story is all true. I've been known to fib gently, but this is all true. I'm not being cheap and I'm not sprucing it up. Really. Not even a little. *Mahsi cho.* Thank you very much. *A ho!*"

After

1. **Reading for Meaning** What have you learned about the Dogrib culture by reading this story? Give details from the story to support this learning.
2. **Reading for Meaning** Why did the family decide to move their camp? Choose the best answer from the choices below.
   A. They didn't want to get attacked by the *Nagha*.
   B. They set up camp too late at night and didn't realize that the land was inhospitable.
   C. They needed to find a better area for hunting.
   D. They wanted to respect the *Nagha* by not camping in his territory.
3. **Reading for Meaning** In the story, the grandmother gives the gift of the moccasins to the *Nagha* as a sign of respect. What are other instances of respect in the story?
4. **Student Voice** Do you believe that the events in the story are possible? Why or why not?
5. **Critical Literacy** What are the key themes in this story? Are these themes demonstrated in your own family? Explain.
6. **Metacognition** Reread the first sentence in the story and think about why the author wrote the story. How does knowing the author's purpose for writing a story enhance your understanding of it?

Beyond

Critical Literacy "The Biggest Moccasins in the World" is told from the author's recollections of stories told to him by his uncle. Write or tell your own version of this story from the perspective of the *Nagha*. How does your version differ?

Story of the Dream Catcher

Essay

Written by Xavier Kataquapit

As a Cree writer, Xavier Kataquapit's stories tell of the people on the land in the area of Attawapiskat First Nation, in northern Ontario, where he was born and raised. In addition to working as a newspaper columnist, his writing has been featured on various Canadian radio broadcast programs.

Before

What do you already know about the meaning and use of dream catchers?

During

As you read this essay, make notes about any new learning you discover about dream catchers.

Tips

Wabun Youth Gathering: an annual event initiated by the Wabun elders and chiefs to provide guidance and encouragement to Wabun youth

***meegwetch*:** thank you [in the Ojibway, Cree, and Oji-Cree languages]

When I was growing up in Attawapiskat, I rarely had the opportunity to learn about Native culture and traditions. We were brought up with a spiritual belief that was really more religious and based on the Roman Catholic faith. The missionaries had brought this belief to the people of the James Bay coast and to Native people right across North and South America. I did not really understand when I was young that it had not always been that way.

It was surprising to me that we had a spiritual way, culture, and traditions before the coming of the Europeans. My elders have been able to tell me something about those days, but most of my learning has come from traditional elders, healers, medicine men, and people who have a more intricate knowledge of the ancestors.

This summer I learned much about dream catchers from Marcia Martel-Brown of Brunswick House First Nation. I met her at the annual Wabun Youth Gathering where she was sharing teachings on the dream catcher. My first knowledge of the dream catcher is similar, I imagine, to most other people. I always thought they were just Native craftwork that had something to do with keeping bad dreams away.

Actually, the true origins of the dream catcher have to do with healing and the complex process that revolved around the making of this item. Marcia explained that our ancestors used the making of the dream catcher as part of a healing journey.

Long ago, when Native people had a better understanding of their own spirituality, culture, and traditions, the dream catcher was an important tool for a community. If someone was feeling emotional or physical pain, he or she might choose to go on a healing journey that involved the making of a dream catcher.

This person would contact a healer or medicine man in the community and ask for assistance on this journey. A person would have to get permission from his or her family because the family would have to survive without the constant presence and help from the person seeking healing. Once there was agreement, the seeker of healing worked closely with the healer to learn the ways of dealing with or healing a hurt.

Marcia explained that this was a very big deal in a community. When someone decided to go on a healing journey and begin making a dream catcher, it was up to the community to support the person and the family. The community would pitch in so that both the person and the family would survive while the journey was taken. The entire community knew about the journey and there was a huge feast to celebrate the decision.

Once the journey started, the person on the healing quest and healer spent much time together. There was no set time limit for this process and sometimes it took seasons and even years to complete. It all started with hunting and gathering to find the items to make a dream catcher. Some of these items included willow branches, sinew, stone, and various other items as decided on by the healer.

They travelled out on the land to hunt and gather what they needed. During this time they spent days and days together discussing the life history of the person on the quest. The dream catcher then started to take form. First, the selected willow branch was bent either to cross or meet in a circle. This represented the person's beginning of life to the present and all that happened in that time. Then slowly the healer helped the person produce the sinew and string it inside the circle like ribbons of time. In the slow and patient construction of the dream catcher, stones and other items would be hooked into the emerging web of sinew. These might represent significant events and perhaps times of pain.

After much time, work, and reflection on life, the person on the dream quest would arrive at a place of learning with a finished dream catcher. This was always the hope. At that point, this part of the healing journey came to an end. A new beginning was celebrated in a ceremony. The dream catcher was burned, and the pain and turmoil that had been hurting the person seeking healing disappeared in the flames.

That last part of Marcia's explanation helped me understand why our people never had proof or evidence of dream catchers from long, long ago. None of them survived as they were given over to an important part of the healing process when they were burned.

So, I say a big *meegwetch* to Marcia for bringing me the story of the dream catcher so that I could in turn tell it to you. I wish you sweet dreams.

After

1. **Reading for Meaning** What is the connection between the dream catcher and the healing journey as explained in this essay?
2. **Reading for Meaning** Do you think your community would benefit from following this tradition of the dream catcher and the healing journey? Why or why not?
3. **Critical Literacy** Why do you think the author wrote this essay?
4. **Metacognition** How does the information you've read in this selection align with what you already know?

Beyond

Student Voice Reflect on your own cultural traditions about healing. Organize this information in the form of poetry, art, artifacts, or music.

Innovations

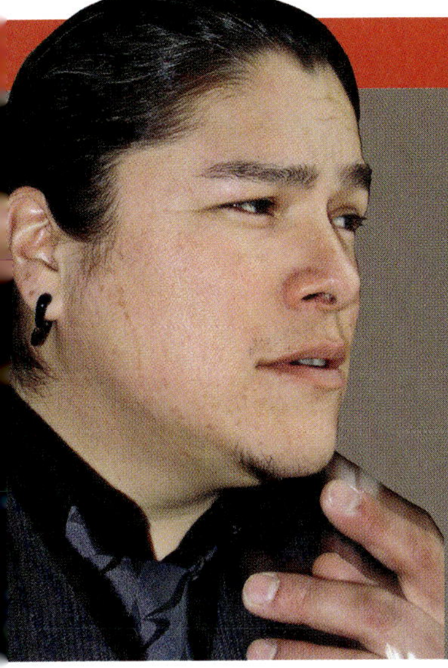

Artwork by Elliott Doxtater-Wynn

Elliott Doxtater-Wynn has a university degree and currently teaches arts and culture in a variety of schools, including preschools and colleges. His art has been included in many exhibitions across Canada. This is how Elliott describes himself: "I am a Mohawk of the Six Nations and Ojibway of Manitoulin Island on Turtle Island. I was raised on the pow-wow trail and taught to dance and hear the heartbeat in the drums by my grandfather. I am part of a new understanding that family is important and that I must protect my beliefs, my family, my friends, my community, our world. I am part of the reclaiming of traditional knowledge. I am part of educating others on how important they are. We are all connected. We are all on the same path. Right and wrong are determined by the direction you are going. I am on the warrior's path, Wasáse, a Jedi."

Before

What do you already know about things invented by First Nations, Inuit, and Métis peoples?

During

As you read, make notes about which innovations interest you the most and what additional information you would like to know.

Before Europeans arrived, First Nations, Métis, and Inuit peoples in Canada invented many technologies for survival, ease of transportation, overcoming the challenges of the environment, cultural cohesion, and enjoyment. These innovations continue to enrich our lives today. Here are some of those innovations.

Kayaks

Inuit ancestors invented kayaks, making them from seal or walrus skins pulled over a wooden frame. They created a special folded seam that helped make the kayaks waterproof. The kayaker was connected to the kayak with a gut-skin apron, which allowed the skilful paddler to complete a "kayak roll" and not take any water inside the kayak. A one-person kayak could cover more than 100 km a day.

Toboggans

The Anishinabe invented toboggans as a way of towing loads over the snow. They could be pulled by people or dogs. Wood was boiled until it could be curved into shape. A strap was attached to the end of the toboggan and could be used as a brake by someone walking behind the sled. Inuit also made toboggans, but out of whale bone.

Snowshoes

First Nations people who lived in cold climates devised technology for walking on top of snow. The style of the snowshoes differed from place to place, depending on the materials available, but all worked by distributing a person's weight across a wider surface to keep him or her from sinking into the snow.

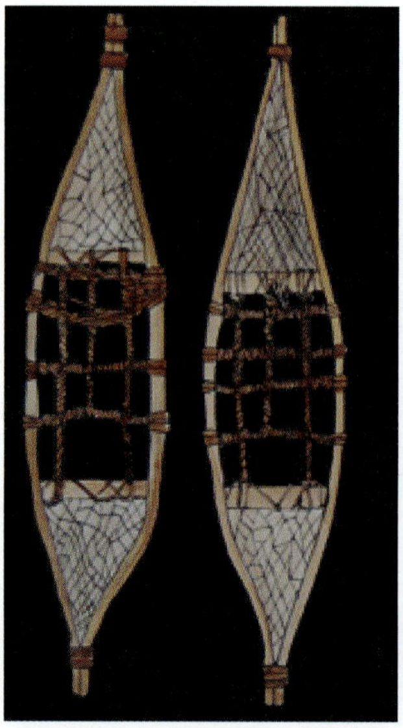

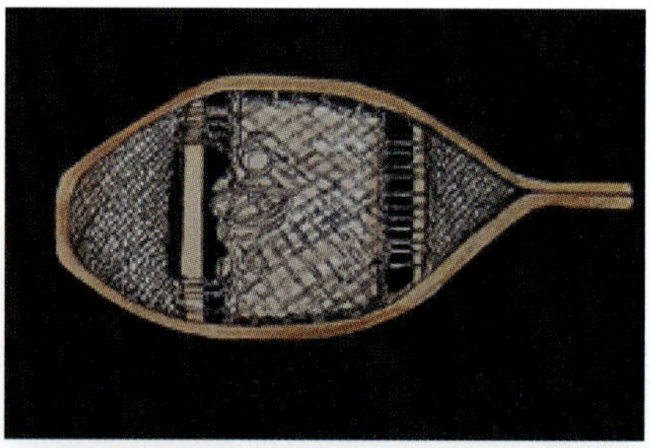

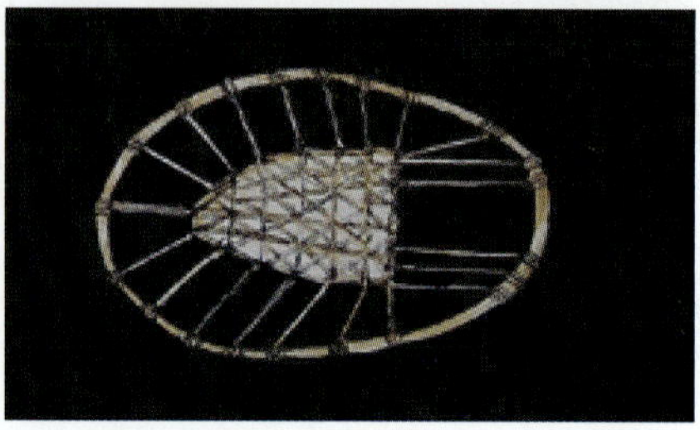

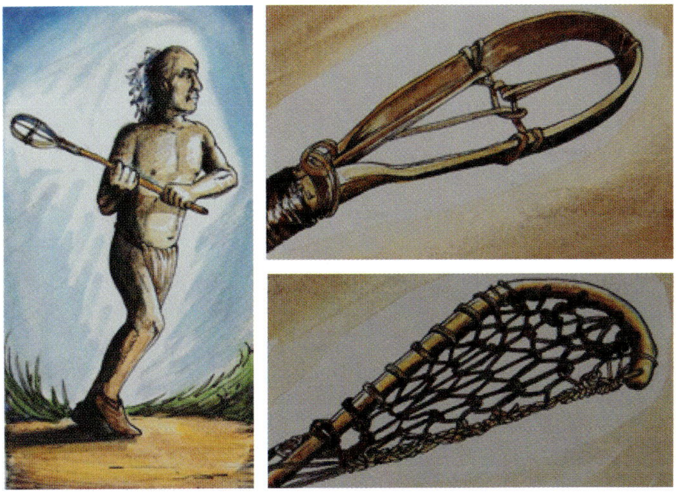

Lacrosse

This game was common among First Nations people throughout North America. Sometimes the game was called "the little brother of war" because it was viewed as a good way to train for battle. As in the modern game, players used long sticks with mesh pockets to carry a ball across a field to score on the opposition's net.

Hockey

Field hockey and ice hockey are both based on the First Nations game of stickball called shinny. It was played mostly by women, who used a wooden or buckskin ball. Players used sticks to move the ball, but also were allowed to use their feet.

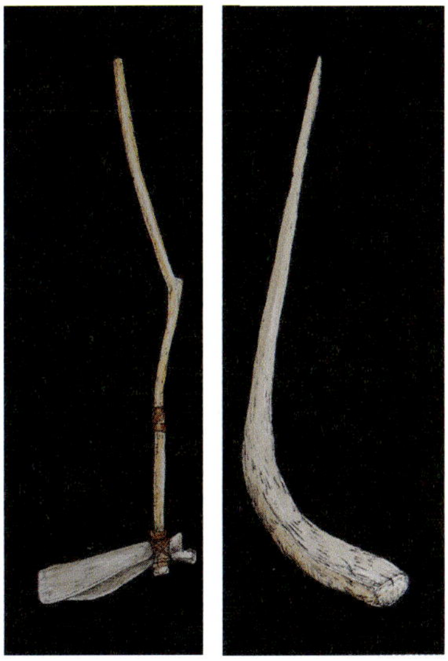

Fish Hooks

First Nations, Inuit, and Métis peoples across North America made hooks attached to lines for catching fish. Sometime between 5000 and 4000 BCE, First Nations people living near the Great Lakes invented what is likely the world's first metal fish hook.

Calendars

Plains peoples used the stars to create a system of gauging the passage of time. Circles of stones were laid out to create "medicine wheels." The spokes in the wheels align with the rising of certain constellations in the night sky. A medicine wheel at Moose Mountain in Saskatchewan is carbon-dated to be 2600 years old.

Pain Relievers and Other Remedies

The active ingredient in some pain relievers used today, such as aspirin, was known to First Peoples in Canada for centuries. This ingredient, found in willow trees, was used to treat bee stings and other ailments. Plains peoples also used another plant called echinacea to treat insect bites. Echinacea has both antiviral and antiseptic properties.

Bunk Beds

Iroquois and Algonkin peoples used bunk beds in their longhouses. The beds were attached to the walls and covered with bark sheeting, then hides and furs. The upper bunks were used for sleeping or storage of personal items.

Maple Syrup

First Nations people in what is now eastern Canada and the United States collected the sap from maple trees and created the technology to transform the liquid into syrup and sugar. It was often used to sweeten dishes made from corn.

After

1. **Reading for Meaning** Choose one innovation. Explain how the modern-day version of this innovation is different from the original innovation.
2. **Metacognition** Describe how the information presented in this selection can be applied in other subject areas.
3. **Critical Literacy** There are many more innovations that can be attributed to First Nations, Inuit, and Métis peoples, such as tipis, longhouses, moccasins, soapstone sculpting, snow houses, and other medicines. Why do you think the innovations shown in this selection were chosen?
4. **Student Voice** Do you think it's important to learn about innovations made by First Nations, Inuit, and Métis peoples? Explain why or why not.

Beyond

Reading for Meaning Choose one innovation that you would like to learn more about. Research this innovation and present your findings in a form of your choice. Be sure to include the ways in which the innovation benefits our lives today.

From Earth to Sky: Everything We Need Is Right Here

Painting

By Christi Belcourt

Christi Belcourt is a visual artist whose Métis ancestry originates from Lac Ste. Anne, Alberta. Christi grew up in Ottawa, Ontario, and currently lives in Noatkamegwanning First Nation near Sioux Narrows, in north-western Ontario. She is a recipient of awards from the Canada Council for the Arts, the Ontario Arts Council, and the Métis Nation of Ontario.

Before

Define the word *spirit*. How does your definition of spirit connect to this piece of art?

During

As you view this piece, think about the emotions this art might evoke.
Who do you think this piece of art was created for?

What Inspired Me to Create This Selection

"This painting was done as a reference for a full-scale beaded work of the same title. From the core of Mother Earth to the infinite universe, all that we need as human beings spiritually is already here. We exist not only in this physical realm, but also in the spiritual realm at the same time. Our spiritual selves exist among, within, and in full partnership with the other spirits that exist in this realm. Spirits are everywhere—within the waters, the plants, the rocks, and by our sides as spirit helpers. The Creator is within each and every one of us. We need not await death in order for the mysteries of our world to be known to us, for what we need is already within and around us. We are more powerful as human beings than we realize because we are complete with all the knowledge of the earth and universe."

After

1. **Student Voice** How would you describe this painting?
2. **Reading for Meaning** Write one question that you would like to ask the artist about the painting. Explain why you chose this question.
3. **Metacognition** How does the title, "From Earth to Sky: Everything We Need Is Right Here," help you understand the painting?
4. **Critical Literacy** Why do you think this piece is important to the artist?
5. **Reading for Meaning** How could this painting be used in a math class or science class?

Beyond

Reading for Meaning Research another Métis, First Nations, or Inuit artist. Create a multi-media presentation or write a magazine article about the artist and his or her artwork. Include a brief explanation on how the style of this artist is different from or similar to Christi Belcourt's.

We said to Inuit, "Tell us your history"

Interview

Interview with Justice James Igloliorte

James Igloliorte spent most of his career as a judge ensuring the Canadian justice system was applied in such a way that it respected the cultures of Inuit, as well as First Nations and Métis peoples. He's been a teacher and a vice-principal, and he was most recently the chief commissioner of the Qikiqtani Truth Commission. This commission investigated the alleged slaughter by the RCMP of thousands of sled dogs over a period of more than twenty years, among other issues still affecting Inuit to this day.

Tip

Qikiqtani Inuit Association: an organization representing the interests of the Inuit of the Baffin Region, High Arctic, and Belcher Islands

Before

Preview the text. Describe the text structure and predict what you think the selection is about.

During

1. As you read, note whether your predictions about the content were confirmed.
2. As you read, consider what additional questions you would have asked Justice Igloliorte if you were interviewing him. Think about the information you would want him to clarify.

Interviewer: What was your upbringing like?
Justice Igloliorte: Well, I grew up in an Inuk family and it wasn't until very close to kindergarten before English was used to any degree, but when we went to school, the provincial education system was entirely done in English. It wasn't long before I was losing my conversational Inuktitut.

Interviewer: Do you regret losing your language?
Justice Igloliorte: Naturally, a loss of any original language is regrettable. Particularly Inuktitut, which is presently threatened in a lot of places, at least in Labrador, simply because of the changing times.

I do regret the loss, but I am working personally to retain what I have.

Interviewer: You graduated from Memorial University in Newfoundland with a Bachelor in Science and Education. How did you make the transition to law?
Justice Igloliorte: I had been a vice-principal in St. James School in Lark Harbour, Newfoundland, for seven years and I could see that our principal wasn't going anywhere. ...

In 1980, I had a call from the Department of Justice asking if I would be interested in and applying for a position as a "lay magistrate." Then I'd have the opportunity to go to law school at Dalhousie University, in Halifax.

My wife and I talked it over, and in July of 1980, I became a lay magistrate, trained in the court system for magistrates in St. John's. In 1982, I attended law school at Dalhousie. I graduated in 1985 with a law degree and went back to the bench as a provincial court judge.

Interviewer: Did you miss being a teacher?
Justice Igloliorte: Not really; I found law a new challenge. Law school was extremely difficult for me. I think it was only through the grace of good, understanding professors at Dalhousie that I got through it. ...

I didn't miss the education side. I found law school and law, criminal law particularly, to be a real challenge.

Interviewer: Can you explain a bit about how you approached law differently from other judges?
Justice Igloliorte: Having come from an Inuit community, and living in a part of Canada where Aboriginal people form the majority of the population, I took a lot of pains to try to explain [to people involved in court cases] what was happening in the legal process and explain legal concepts as much as I could.

The very concept of having charges [laid] against you by police, having to go through a process where those charges must be proven, and the concept that [you have] the right to remain silent were absolutely foreign to people who were used to a system of community justice. The Canadian justice system was strange to them. It was very important to try to make people understand that it was a transition process, and the way they thought about law, breaking the law, and community transgressions, was going to be treated differently than before.

I encouraged lawyers to enjoy working with their clients and not to see them as offenders but as individuals, and to try to work in such a way that people understood that they were respected despite the fact that they might have been in trouble.

The justice system at the time had very little room for that kind of respect for people's rights. When they had transgressed against a fellow member, Aboriginal people ordinarily would have been given a chance [by the community] to try and return to some form of harmony with that individual. But instead, there was a state system, which was stepping in and saying, "No, we have a formal process, and it doesn't allow you to deal personally and individually through your community with the person you have victimized."

Instead there was a whole new process, which took away the community's responsibility and gave it to the state, so that was a huge difference in people's perceptions of law. That's something I continued to work on and tried to encourage [non-Aboriginal] lawyers to look at through the perspective of the Aboriginal person.

Interviewer: Most recently, you were chief commissioner for the Qikiqtani Truth Commission. What did the commission find?

Justice Igloliorte: Essentially, the Qikiqtani Inuit Association told us to conduct a process that would emphasize reconciliation between the federal government and Inuit, and not [focus too much on] the RCMP's alleged killing of dogs. We put [the killing of dogs] in a context of what the federal government's responsibilities should have been at the time. How they acted and how they fell short of their duty in issues of health care, education, and community involvement—people should have had a lot

of dialogue and consultation before decisions were made. So we expanded what was called a "dog slaughter issue" into an historical overview of the time period and then a critical analysis of what the federal government was required to do. It became a much broader theme than just looking at the dog-slaughter issue.

Interviewer: What were those larger issues?
Justice Igloliorte: There was a period between about 1950 and 1975 when the federal government was treating Aboriginal people across Canada very much the same way as Aboriginal people were being treated worldwide: there was a huge move toward centralization of services so that Inuit, who were nomadic people living in small bands of one or two families throughout the entire Baffin Island region, were forced through various federal government policies and programs to live in what are now thirteen communities in the same region. Inuit went from 100 communities down to 13, in a period of about 20 or 25 years.

And what occurred, of course, is that if people wanted to have their $6 a month family allowance, then they had to send their children to school. If the children had to go to school, then these places had to be built, which started the moving of Inuit people's homes into communities that had no relationship to where the land could provide for them. The bringing together of so many people in a small area resulted in hunters having no ability to practise their skills. And this whole change to community lifestyle brought health changes as well.

The transition period was very traumatic for the people that we studied. We started with no preconceptions. We said to Inuit, "Tell us your history. Tell us what you remember. Tell us what bothers you." And we used that information to have researchers look through the various archives from the RCMP, archives from Health Canada, archives from the various governments at the time, and find out what the federal government was thinking and writing and doing in the form of programs and consultation. Our report very much examined the activities of the federal government and the impact on Inuit today.

Interviewer: How did you feel, hearing these painful memories?
Justice Igloliorte: We had people who had lived through that period, whose first thought was for the loss of their dogs and the culture of having used dogs and dog teams to survive. They felt that if it were not for dog teams, they would not have survived as long as they did, as Inuit. It was a special relationship, existing nowhere else in any culture in the world between humans and teams of dogs.

The government's response to moving so many people into communities and so many dogs into communities was to say, "These dogs are dangerous, they form packs, and as a consequence they should be killed whenever they come to the communities."

The Inuit were confused by these laws, which applied to farms in the south where maybe a bad dog would be killing animals. [The government] applied laws that mirrored that kind of thinking rather than saying to Inuit, "How can we work with you to preserve your culture?"

Instead, they applied a law that said dogs had to be chained. Well, there were no chains and they chewed through harnesses and ropes. The Canadian law said, "'If you don't retrieve your dog within six hours or so many days, they will be shot. If we can't catch your dogs, we will shoot them."

Inuit said, "This was a very traumatic period for us, and it affects how we think about the past." They came to us, in many cases, in very emotional states, saying, "Finally, we have had a chance to tell about how we feel, how the official government process worked, and how it has affected us and our relationships with our families to have undergone such a tremendous change in a short time."

These were, I think, things that would pull at anybody's heartstrings who had to sit down and listen to individual stories repeated time after time after time. We began to see the pattern of how many people were affected. We could show the Inuit in communities 600 miles apart that the same thing was happening to other Inuit. It was not a unique situation.

Interviewer: What kind of response has there been to the Commission's findings?
Justice Igloliorte: The response from the Qikiqtani Inuit Association has been extremely good. We've recommended that they complete our work by finishing a video

project of the entire process. And we're saying that, when the entire book is written and translated into Inuktitut, it should be presented to the Parliament of Canada. It would let Canada know that there are many issues that Inuit and the federal government and Inuit governments have to work on together.

I think the day is coming when the entire package will be put to Canadians and they will have a chance to look at this history, but it's not a fast process. We have always chosen to work in the reconciliation process to try to mend bridges and get people to acknowledge, first of all, that this happened. After the acknowledgment is when the next steps will kick in.

After

1. **Metacognition** How did thinking about questions you want answered help you analyze and understand the selection?
2. **Reading for Meaning** Explain how the alleged slaughter of sled dogs by the RCMP is representative of larger issues concerning Inuit rights and the loss of their traditional way of life.
3. **Critical Literacy** Whose perspectives are not included in this interview? Why do you think they weren't included?
4. **Critical Literacy** With whom do you think Justice Igloliorte wants us to identify or sympathize? Explain, using evidence from the selection.

Beyond

1. **Student Voice** Two reports were completed based on the government's inquiry into the allegations of the slaughter of Inuit sled dogs by the RCMP. One is the Qikiqtani Truth Commission report, which Justice Igloliorte was involved in. The other is the RCMP report, called *Final Report: RCMP Review of Allegations Concerning Inuit Sled Dogs*.
   a) Locate these reports on the Internet and summarize their findings.
   b) How are the reports the same?
   c) How are the reports different? What might account for the differences?
   d) Taking these perspectives into consideration, what are your conclusions about the allegations of the slaughter of sled dogs?

2. **Listening and Speaking** Select an issue in your community that involves relations between people in the community and the police or local or provincial government. Choose two people who have different views on the issue. Prepare a list of questions for each person and interview them. Be sure to record your interviews.

Heroes

Rap Lyrics

Written by Wab Kinew

Wab Kinew has won an Aboriginal Peoples Choice Music Award for his hip-hop music and an imagineNATIVE Film + Media Arts Festival award and New York Festivals Finalist certificate for his journalism at the CBC. He was also nominated for a Future Leaders of Manitoba award in 2010. He has a BA in economics and has training in the traditional medicine ways of his Anishnabe people.

Before

Reflect on the title of the rap and look at the photo on the opposite page. What connections do you make between the two?

During

As you read, make a list of all the heroes the writer mentions. Highlight the heroes you have not heard of before.

Tips

sun dance: a spiritual ceremony practised among First Nations peoples, marked by several days of fasting and group dancing

***kookum*:** grandmother [in the Oji-Cree and Cree languages]

I hear a lot of people say the Native community needs heroes ... well, we already have our heroes so let's just take a minute to remember them.

How did Louis Riel become a buffalo soldier?
Stood up to Canada, the father of Manitoba.
How did Fontaine get the apology?
He told his story then he said come on follow me.
That's the gift. I guess I'll pass it on,
like the teachings passed at the sun dance before dawn.
How did Waneek take a knife to the ribs,
then represent this country? Damn, she forgives.
And how does Leonard Peltier get out of bed each day?
Finding hope in the hopeless it's the Indian way.
And why did Tommy Prince fight for all Canadian people,
when right here at home he wasn't considered an equal?
Overseas he fought with the heart of a warrior
then came back home to be treated like a foreigner.
So yeah, I'm a live real lavish
for all the times you called my people savage.

How did Kateri know that she should keep up the faith?
Time to put the first Native saint in her proper place.
How did Buffy St. Marie know to keep on singing?
"Bury My Heart At Wounded Knee" it keeps on ringing.
How did Freddy Krueger know he had to stand up?
Since I saw the photo knew I had to man up.

How did Peguis know he should help that white man?
Did he understand others would take his land?
But damn, the worst is over now.
The bro Adam Beach is on movie posters now.
This is big Wab, still reppin' the Rez.
Though I'm in the city no I won't soon forget
what the elders taught me: Always to share.
My people don't want the pride? Well, I don't care.
How did K'naan know the world need this song?
Well, I'll never know the answer so I just sing along like ...

Yeahhhhhhhhh, some true Native heroes right there.
If you haven't heard about them, learn about them.
I'd tell you to go read a book about them but they don't write about our heroes in the history books.
So go ask an elder, go ask Grandma, go ask Kookum.
Better yet ask Wab Kinew.
I've got opinions for days.
Gladly talk your ear off.
And this is just the beginning.
This could be a 500 bar song.
One bar for every year of oppression, one bar for every rhyme I got to make an impression ... on today's youth.

Canadian soldier Patrick Cloutier and Brad Larocque, known as Freddy Krueger, come face to face on September 1, 1990, during the Oka Crisis. The Oka Crisis was a land dispute between the Mohawk community of Kanesatake and the town of Oka, Quebec.

What Inspired Me to Write This Selection

"My inspiration arose when speaking to my kickboxing coach. He's non-Native but works with a lot of Aboriginal kids. He said that the Native community is in need of heroes, which led me to think that we have a ton of great heroes—they're just not recognized or celebrated enough. So I decided to celebrate them in a piece."

After

1. **Critical Literacy** Who would be most likely to listen to this rap? Do you think the intended audience influenced the way the writer wrote it?
2. **Reading for Meaning** Do you think this rap is effective in delivering its message? Why or why not?
3. **Student Voice** How does your own definition of heroes compare with the writer's idea of heroes as presented in this rap?
4. **Understanding Form and Style** What stylistic elements make this selection a rap?
5. **Metacognition** What strategies did you use to make sense of the rap?

Beyond

Listening and Speaking Select one of the heroes the writer mentions. Research this person and present your findings to the class in a form of your choice.

Glossary of Literary Terms

A

alliteration: the deliberate repetition of sounds or syllables, especially initial consonants, for stylistic effect

allusion: a brief reference, explicit or implicit, to a place, person, or event

analogy: a comparison of two elements from different categories in order to shed light on one or both elements

anthropomorphism: giving human characteristics to something that is not human, such as an animal or inanimate object. The author's use of anthropomorphism in *The Animal People Choose a Leader* is characteristic of traditional First Nations, Inuit, and Métis storytelling.

C

caption: a title or brief explanation that accompanies an illustration or photo and usually explains the content or purpose of the image

collage: a form of art in which a variety of materials, such as photographs, fabric, objects, and printed text are attached to a surface

critical literacy: looking beyond the literal meaning of text to observe what is present and what is missing, in order to analyze and evaluate the text's complete meaning and the author's intent

critical thinking: the process of thinking about ideas or situations in order to understand them fully, identify their implications, and/or make a judgment about what is sensible or reasonable to believe or do

D

dash (—): longer than a hyphen, can be used like commas or parentheses to set off a parenthetical remark or aside. Dashes sometimes set off text that the author wants to emphasize.

E

essay: a short composition in which a point is made, usually through analysis and example

F

figurative language or figures of speech: descriptive and often poetic devices in which meaning is concentrated and heightened, usually through comparison

first-person narrative: a story narrated by one character, using the words "I" (first-person singular) and "we" (first-person plural) and representing a point of view

foreshadowing: a literary device in which an author suggests developments or events that might occur later in the story

form: structure or organization of a text

G

genres: types or categories of text recognized by form and/or style; for example, essay, article, documentary, Web page, short story, graphic novel, poem

graphic organizer: a visual by which the relationships between and among ideas are portrayed; for example, a Venn diagram, T-chart, web

I

imagery: use of sensory details to evoke a mental picture

irony: a manner of expression in which a statement that seems literally to mean one thing actually means another

italics: used to draw attention to a particular part of the text and provide emphasis. They can also be used for contrast, to denote titles, and for foreign words.

J

juxtaposition: the act of placing items or ideas side by side for comparison or contrast

L

literary device: deliberate use of language to create a particular effect; for example, allusion, flashback, foreshadowing, imagery, symbolism, metaphor, simile

M

metacognition: "thinking about thinking," which results in students' individual knowledge of their own learning processes

metaphor: a comparison of two items not usually seen as similar, but without using the words *like* or *as*. In *E5-770, My Mother's Name*, the author uses *cattled* and *farmed* to compare the treatment of her mother to the treatment of cattle.

N

novella: a short novel

P

personification: a figure of speech in which a nonhuman object is described as human

Q

quotation marks (" "): identify the start and finish of spoken dialogue in a story

S

sensory details: description that appeals to any of the five senses (sight, sound, taste, smell, touch)

simile: a comparison made using the words *like* or *as*

square brackets [ ]: sometimes used to clarify information in direct quotations. In *Protect Our Land: A Chief's Perspective*, the author often uses square brackets to clarify text quoted by Chief Donny Morris.

stanza: a grouping of lines in a poem, set off by a space

stereotype: an image or understanding of a particular type of person or thing that has become fixed through being widely held. Stereotypes are usually conventional, formulaic, and oversimplified.

symbol: one thing that stands for another, as in a flag representing a country. Symbols in word form appear frequently in poetry, drama, fiction, and essays.

T

text features: the physical or design characteristics of a text that clarify and/or give support to the meaning in the text; for example, title, headings, subheadings, bold and italic fonts

text form: a category or type of text that has certain defining characteristics. The concept of text forms provides a way for readers and writers to think about the purpose of a text and its intended audience.

third-person narrator: a person who is not a character in the story and who tells the story from that perspective

V

voice: the individuality of the writer as perceived by the reader

Glossary of First Nations, Métis, and Inuit Terms

A

Aboriginal peoples: the original inhabitants of North America and their descendants. The Canadian Constitution recognizes three groups of Aboriginal people: First Nations, Métis, and Inuit.

***ajaaja*:** a traditional Inuit song, often involving stories about people and their travels

Aleut: native to the Aleutian Islands and coastal areas of southwestern Alaska

Anishnaabe (also spelled Anishinaabe, Anishinabe, Anishnabe depending on the community, or Anishinabek/Anishinabeg in the plural form): one of the largest First Nations groups in North America; also called Ojibway in Canada or Chippewa in the United States.

C

cultural genocide: the deliberate destruction of the cultural heritage of a people for political, military, religious, ideological, ethnic, or racial reasons

culture: the way in which people live, think, and define themselves as a community

D

Dogrib: First Nations peoples who live in the Great Slave Lake area of the Northwest Territories

F

First Nations peoples: a collective term for Aboriginal peoples who are not Inuit or Métis. Many communities have also adopted the term *First Nation* to replace the word *band*. International law recognizes a *nation* as a distinct group or race of people that share history, traditions, and culture, and says that a *nation* is entitled to self-government. The term *First Nation* was adopted during the struggle by First Nations peoples to be recognized as distinct societies in Canada.

First Peoples: a collective term for First Nations, Métis, and Inuit peoples in Canada, as well as indigenous peoples around the world

H

holistic wheel: (also known as the medicine wheel) a circle divided into four sections that each represent a direction (east, south, west, and north), as well as seasons, calendar months, race, gifts, age, and personal development. It is a symbol of harmony and peaceful interaction among all living beings on earth.

I

Indian: this word has a legal meaning in Canadian law and refers to Aboriginal people who are not Inuit or Métis. Many First Nations people find this term offensive and prefer to be identified more accurately by the name of their own community, (e.g., St'at'imc person, Tsilhqot'in Nation) or collectively as Aboriginal, First Nations, Native, or Indigenous people.

***Indian Act*:** a set of laws first passed by the Canadian government in 1876 and still enforced today, although the act has undergone many changes. It regulates the relationship between First Nations peoples and Canada, including government, education, health services, land, tax, and legal matters.

indigenous: means "native to the area." Aboriginal peoples are indigenous to North America. Its meaning is similar to Aboriginal peoples, Native peoples, or First Peoples.

infinity symbol: symbolizes the joining of two cultures and the existence of a people forever. The infinity symbol appears on the Métis flag.

Inuit: Aboriginal peoples who live in Arctic Canada, primarily in Nunavut, the Northwest Territories, and northern parts of Labrador and Quebec

K

***Kitchi-Manitou*:** the Creator [in Ojibway tradition]

***kookum*:** grandmother or grandma [in the Oji-Cree and Cree languages]

M

***mahsi cho*:** thank you very much [in the Dogrib language]

***meegwetch*:** thank you [in the Ojibway, Cree, and Oji-Cree languages]

medicine man: a person who acts as a bridge between the natural and spirit worlds, and seeks help from the spirit world for healing, divination, and control over natural events

medicine wheel: (also known as the holistic wheel) a circle divided into four sections that each represent a direction (east, south, west, and north), as well as seasons, calendar months, race, gifts, age, and personal development. It is a symbol of harmony and peaceful interaction among all living beings on earth.

Métis: people of mixed First Nations and European descent who identify themselves as Métis. Some Métis people make a distinction between those who can trace their ancestry back to the Red River Valley in Manitoba, and those that can't.

***mishom*:** short form for *mishomis*, which means grandfather [in the Ojibway language]

N

***Nagha* (Sasquatch):** a very large, hairy, humanlike creature said to live in remote wilderness areas of Canada and the United States

NDN: a play on the word *Indian*, used often on social networking sites, such as Facebook and Twitter, and in texting

P

pow-wow: a social, cultural, and often spiritual gathering of First Nations peoples (sometimes including Inuit and Métis people) where drumming, dancing, and regalia are often showcased

pow-wow grass dance: a form of men's dancing at a pow-wow involving colourful regalia that resembles a field in motion. The grass dance documents the journey of a man preparing land to camp in a respectful way.

R

residential schools: boarding schools run mainly from the 1830s to the 1950s to educate First Nations, Métis, and Inuit children and erase their traditional languages and cultures. Students were often forcibly removed from their homes and families and subjected to abuse in these schools.

S

shaking tent: a traditional sacred ceremony practised by many First Nations peoples, which involves invoking spirits to assist and answer questions

sun dance: a spiritual ceremony practised among First Nations peoples, marked by several days of fasting and group dancing

sweetgrass: one of four sacred medicines that are used to give thanks and to purify space and self with positive energy

sweat lodge: a structure used to induce sweating for medicinal or spiritual purposes

T

tobacco: a traditional medicine that is offered as a gift to the earth or elder

totem poles: monumental sculptures carved from large trees, usually western red cedar, by First Nations peoples of the Pacific Northwest Coast of North America

treaty: a legal agreement between the government of Canada and a First Nation that defines their relationship and establishes rights to land and other resources

treaty card: also known as Status card; an identification card issued by the Canadian government for Status Indians

***Tribal Trails*:** a Christian-based First Nations TV show

two-spirit person: a person born one sex who fulfils the roles assigned to both sexes, or other roles reserved for two-spirit people. Some people consider two-spirit a term that can refer to lesbian, gay, bisexual, and transgender people. The definition of a two-spirit person varies across First Nations, Inuit, and Métis cultures.

Photo and Art Credits

East: First Perspectives

pp. 2–3: Shaun Lowe/Getty Images; pp. 4–16 © The EagleSpeaker Connection; p. 18: © Jackie Hanna; p. 19: Martin Diebel/Getty Images; p. 20: © Hans Strand/Corbis; p. 21: Photographic Services at the Banff Centre; p. 22: *Confessions to the Moon* © Andy Everson; p. 25: © Joyce Hunter; p. 26: *Reach for Your Dreams* © Moses (Amik) Beaver; p. 30: Ken Usami/Getty Images.

South: Sharing Our Gifts

pp. 32–33: © Wayne Lynch/All Canada Photos/Corbis; p. 34: photo provided by Joseph Boyden; p. 36: Bill Hinton Photography/Getty Images; p. 38: © Melanie McLaren; pp. 39–44: photos provided by Nadia McLaren; p. 46: Toronto Star/GetStock.com; p. 48: R/G Photography in Prince Albert, Saskatchewan; p. 49: The EagleSpeaker Connection; p. 50: © Shaun Manchester; pp. 51-54: The EagleSpeaker Connection; p. 58: © Kai Zyganiuk; p. 60: © Kai Zyganiuk; p. 62: © Margie Faccini-Lee; p. 63: *Grandmother Spider Connects All Life Together* © Aaron Paquette; p. 66: © Nadya Kwandibens; p. 68: Adrienne Fox & Brent Wesley.

West: Taking a Stand

pp. 70–71: Stephen Strathdee/Getty Images; p. 72: Stephan Hoglund Photography; p. 73: *Young Couple* © Jim Logan; p. 74: photo provided by Richard Wagamese; pp. 75–80: Kristy Cameron; p. 83: reprinted with permission from SEVEN Youth Media Network; p. 85: The Chronicle-Journal-Brent Linton/Canadian Press; p. 87: top: Wawatay News, bottom: reprinted with permission from SEVEN Youth Media Network; p. 93: © Chris Bose; pp. 94–95: © Nadya Kwandibens; p. 96: Steward Kasdorf; p. 97: *Buffalo Woman* © Aaron Paquette; pp. 98–99: courtesy of Ronald Everett Green; p. 101: © Aaron Pierre; p. 102: Tom Hanson/Canadian Press; p. 104: Mike Dembeck/Canadian Press; p. 106: J.P. Moczulski/Canadian Press; p. 108: TRC; p. 110: John Woods/Canadian Press.

North: The People's Wisdom

pp. 112–113: Frank Lukasseck/Getty Images; p. 115: © Chris Bose; p. 116: © Marci Becking; p. 117: photo by Luis Machinho courtesy of the *Anishinabek News*, published by the Union of Ontario Indians; p. 118: photo by Nicole Latulippe courtesy of the *Anishinabek News*, published by the Union of Ontario Indians; p. 120: © Mark Mushett; pp. 121–122: Moses (Amik) Beaver; p. 124: courtesy of Xavier Kataquapit, photo by Mike McGrath; p. 125: Alain/Dreamstime.com; p. 127–131: Elliott Doxtater-Wynn; p. 132: © Jeanna Pelletier; p. 133: *From Earth to Sky: Everything We Need is Right Here* © Christi Belcourt; p. 134: photo provided by James Igloliorte; 136: Alexandra Kobalenko/All Canada Photos; p. 138: Doug Allan/Getty Images; p. 140: © Anthony "Thosh" Collins; p. 141: Shaney Komulainen/Canadian Press; p. 142: top left: Eric Liebowitz/NBC/NBCU Photo Bank/Canadian Press, bottom left: Toronto Star/GetStock.com, centre: CP PHOTO/Winnipeg Free Press-Jeff De Booy, right: Manitoba Archives/Canadian Press.

Text Credits

All material is reproduced by permission of the author except the following:

"Truth and Reconciliation" by Justice Murray Sinclair reproduced by permission of The Truth and Reconciliation Commission.

The text for "Innovations" by Elliott Doxtater-Wynn was based on information from the following sources:
Encyclopedia of American Indian Contributions to the World by Emory Dean Keoke and Kay Marie Porterfield, Facts on File, Inc. Copyright 2002.
Aboriginal Innovations in Arts, Sciences, and Technology Handbook: A Public Education Initiative of Lakehead University, the Lakehead University Students Association, and the Department of Indian and Northern Affairs Canada by Buffy Sainte-Marie, et al. Copyright 2000.